An Eastern Tailwii

Across India by bike

By Jack Few

Thank you to the countless kind and encouraging people along the way. To my family, Les, Yvonne and Amie for their constant encouragement and the incredible people that are now in my life forever, I dedicate this book to you all.

भारत मेरे दिल में रहती है
'India lives in my heart'

Late for Work

'In what does the alienation of labour consist? First, that the work is external to the worker, that it is not part of his nature, that consequently he does not fulfill himself in his work but denies himself' - Karl Marx

6:15am. My alarm goes off and I start to get ready for work, I feel pretty miserable, drained and unexcited about the day ahead. I pack my bag, straighten my tie and run out the house towards the train station. I'm already a few minutes late and I start to get frustrated with myself for not getting up earlier, my shirt starts sticking to my back with the sweat and the pressure. Today's a busy day, I have clients to meet, several tedious meetings and long conversations with people I'd rather not say anything to.

On the train I pass beautiful English countryside, flicker past dense woodland and sweep past farms, rivers and sheep mowing the hills in the sunrise. I scroll through my travel playlist on my phone and I'm instantly taken back to the land of previous travels and I start reveling in the memories of being back on a beach in Thailand, threading mountain tracks on a motorbike in Vietnam, moon gazing from a beach hut in Cambodia.
The romantic thoughts quickly fade, and I'm drawn back into the real world, the train stops and spits out a long hydraulic sigh. I feel a great detachment from myself, like all the

important and wise things that I had learned from around the world and its people had fallen into evanescence, classed somehow as artificial, unrealistic, childish. I had developed and established what I thought was such a powerful grip on the world and how I wanted to play my part in it, a role full of adventure, travel, creative community, cultural learning, but as I stepped off the train and towards the office blocks that I'd be sat in for most of the day, I felt like they were all just silly ideas, ideals, immature realities fading further and further away.

Maybe it's immaturity, or just my low tolerance threshold, but the repetitive work routine weighs on my soul and saps the energy from me like a life-sucking mosquito. It makes me want to run, to commit to the calling of adventure that manifests itself in my everyday life. I sit typing up my Monday morning emails and catch my reflection in the dark patches of the screen monitor, my alter ego, shouting at me through the computer, 'get out of here, you're wasting your valuable time, go go go!'.

In my zest for adventure I agreed to turn my back on a lot of structural qualities that framed my current life, security, comfort, good money, from the arms of assured career success, from predictability, from a life that could've easily been drawn out beyond me in a rigid, horizontal line. Instead I would trade it all in for simplicity, adventure, perspective and impracticality. I just didn't see the appeal of working like a mule all week, and getting drunk on the weekend as making the most out of my time.

And by virtue of my escape I would at least, by the bold and feverish surges of excitement that I once felt, experience the wholehearted liberation and impenetrable feeling of freedom I so desperately craved.

*

I crave adventure in every sense. Every evening after work the story stews and thickens, ratchets under my skin. A formidable urge deepens and expands, filling my mind with notions of escape and a craving for being footloose. I would walk for hours around my small town, toying with visions of being in some far away country, on a big adventure, with the breeze at my feet, staring beautiful strangers in the eyes and feasting on new experiences, swimming in a lake, diving off a cliff, cooking over an open fire, meaningful, remote, isolated, purposeful visions. The sort of sensations that every man and woman feel when they start to be pulled, unbridled towards an unknown horizon.

The thirst for adventure becomes stronger, more powerful, more meaningful, more of a calling. I find myself daydreaming new scenarios, it's my imaginative movie that washes over my mind day and night. More whispers appear in the mirrors and other reflections, more confirmations that this orthodox life in not for me, and that I wanted to exchange it all in for more. I would often picture myself there in some far distant place, beaming a huge grin and feeling strong and full of vitality, storming some battered mountain track on my bike surrounded by eminent snowcapped peaks, and fresh alpine air hitting the base of my lungs.

*

It's easy to forget when I'm engaged in my daily errand running and menial tasks that in just a few weeks I'll be jumping on a plane, heading thousands of miles from home and all that's familiar, towards the biggest adventure of my life so far! I'm part bricking it and part alive with spine-tingling excitement!

I'm relishing in the knowledge that I'll soon be traveling by myself on a bike across India, reading books, drinking chai and taking photos. Writing thoughts and experiences down, real learning, and meeting a wonderful slice of India's vast inhabitants. I was about to test myself in the best way possible and enroll in the most important learning experience yet.
An enchanting adventure lay ahead of me. I would travel at a steady pace, in a wild country of mountains and deserts, where success will be measured in miles and new experiences and I'll get to know the country I pass through intimately.

I was about to trade it all in for simplicity, for a life on the open road, living by my means and carrying all that I will need for the next six months on my bike in order to survive, to thrive. It would be my sweaty, dirty and totally liberating penance to the comfort and docile life of a 9-5 office job.

An insatiable wave of excitement and nerve burst through me, chilling me to my bones.

The World of Opposites

'He covered his life with a veil of vagueness, while behind his quiet eyes a rich full life went on' - *J. Steinbeck*

Work

A late train, a paranoid watch, white walls, and empty rooms. Handshakes and fictional affection, small talk and gossip. The smell of bleach and cleaning products, fresh paint and printer ink. Grey floors, grey suits, alien talks with alien men. Bottled water, coffee sachets, office blocks, hourly meetings, green fields on the horizon, quite distant, incessant rings, quarrelling clients and stressed out voices. Despondent, blank talks, 'Are you ok, Jack?', late for the train, more suits, no faces, reading screens, flipping charts, 'Yeh I'm fine', home, cook, drink, forget, turn off, flashing images and white noise, news, sleep, wake, repeat, morning. Late train, a paranoid watch, white walls…

India

Tent down, sunrise, glorious stretch, eat, unfamiliar flavours, push off, new place, jade coloured rivers, fresh fruit from the market, eagles, camels, pine scented cliffs and sunbeams through the forest. Spices, rubbish, shoeless people with beaming smiles, hugs and open ears, encouragement, adrenaline, challenge and perspective, health, open road, a purple curtain drapes over the sky, milky stars and warm breath vapour in cold mountain air. Mountain peaks of snow dipped in gold, cold hands warmed by wood fire and books read by torch light, silence, solitude, head space, peacefulness, spring water from the neck of a mountain, tranquility, euphoria, elation, living with risk and spontaneity, making it up as I go, GO!, sunset, monkeys cleaning their tales in the amber light of dusk, new food, beer, travellers, 'on a bike?'. Tent up, sunrise, glorious stretch, push off...

People

'Whatever you can do or dream you can, begin it. Boldness has genius, power, and magic in it. Begin it now' - Goethe

While I was still in England, I had a wonderful connection with a visitor at work. Jo, was in her mid-fifties and was anchored by some very nomadic quality, she had a fresh, wise shine in her eyes. She was well traveled, rosary beads hung around her slender neck, her eyes were green and bright, the lines around them were drawn upwards from years of smiling.

Speaking with Jo brimmed with comfort and relief having talked to someone who knew what I was craving, it was almost as if she could see it in my eyes. I spoke softly yet giddily about my dreams of heading off to India, about the cycling trip, about travel. She knew this wasn't where I should be, that this wasn't a fertile environment for a young adventurer. She spoke with such knowledge, she spoke from a place that was well versed and experienced in life's flow. I felt an immediate inspired connection. When you find that in a person, even if you've only met briefly, they become part of the family in which you find confirmation, support and encouragement in the light of what you truly want to be doing with your life.

Something else I was desperate to explore real, worldly people from all corners of the globe. So many bad and ignorant stigmas are attached to entire races, cultures, religions, most of it being generated by the news and what we read in the mainstream media. I was fed up and filled to the brim with all the bland stereotypes that surrounded me and forced entire cultures into negative light. There seemed to be a general consensus growing the world is full of increasingly dangerous places filled dangerous people. This cynicism is lazy, the negativity is stupid. I wanted to see the real people of India, of Pakistan, of Israel, of Syria and I knew that India invited such people.

I cycle briefly through the lives of many people. Worldly people, rich, wise, poor, travelling, crazy, inspiring, loving, clueless, ambitious. Each of them on their own cycle. I dip into their lives momentarily and sometimes take with me their stories, our experience, and their encouragement with me. Just the idea is beautiful, to start a fresh day having no idea who I'll meet today, but knowing they will change my experience in some way whether big or small. This journey will put many beautiful people in front of me, people who I wouldn't have met if I hadn't chosen to travel by bike, and the level of gratitude I feel now as a result is tremendous.

*

A young Israeli girl, an ex-soldier, sat alone in a café with her feet curled up under the table, one slightly resting on the other, a small ring blushed gold on her middle toe, she was surrounded by candle light. Some musicians in the corner started to play Tablas and Djembes, a few western girls sang long, high pitch mantras filled the room with ambiance and someone started an enchanting melody on a Sitar. I swallowed the sounds down in breathless mouthfuls resting my back on a wall awash with golden candlelight and a hand painted portrait of Lord Shiva.

The girl was incredibly beautiful; she had warm, healing eyes and a soft incandescent glow. Her long dark hair was pulled over one shoulder. When she spoke, her eyebrows were very mobile and emotive. She lit the end of a spliff, leant against the graffitied wall and wrapped her shawl around her shoulders, smoking alone to the music.

Across the room were three young men, cladded in bohemian drapery with Persian looking shawls and leather waistcoats. The three of them talking was a beautiful sight. The way they sat next to each other, crouched and leaning in and resting their arms on the other's shoulders and touching their palms in agreement, smiling into each other keeping eye contact all the while. One of them pressed his hand against his chest and then touched the other's heart, they nodded and continued to converse calmly for a while, hugged and then separated. It was a beautiful sign of brotherhood, three men possibly from different backgrounds, bound and sharing stories surrounded by beautiful music. It was fairly common scene in these parts, but it touched me deeply, the kindness and close connection with strangers was prevalent throughout India.

Through this great variety of people that I met, the conversations with people would range from the generic to the introvert, 'What is your religion? Are you married? What is your countries currency? Do you play cricket? What do you know about Krishna? Are you a Christian? What is your star sign? Do you know of Osho, Maharajji, or Goenka? Most of which would reignite some obvious questions that I didn't even consider.

In a hostel, a Canadian woman with soft piercing eyes and smooth bronzed skin asked me, 'what will you do next with this energy?'. Her hair was frizzy and braided with beads and she wore a constant smile of enthusiasm. She would prod at my story and question me relentlessly, plying my deeper purposes for doing it. She challenged me and conjured up a discourse about the future that I'd never truly thought about before. Should drove me onto an encouraging wave of thought, fuelling ideas of a life that would see me set out further into the world on two wheels, continuing and extending into this new, adventurous and exhilarating way of life. She confirmed I wasn't crazy, and would chuckle sweetly whenever she did and that this was the story I was meant to tell. She confirmed the reality of this new way of life. To learn from my elders on this trip was a quintessential stage, a vitally important step along the path of learning.

*

I met a young Indian man named Supreet in Rishikesh, he ran a small coffee shop down one of the many rabbit warren, narrow alleyways, past red, fading walls and children peeking out from the high windows. He eyes were as green as the deep Ganga river, his soft jaw coated with a short black beard and his limp shoulders upheld a baggy jumper and silk scarf. He was born and raised as an India, but his engagement with westerners and the music influences that they brought resulted in some of the most beautiful music that I had ever heard. He played some battered looking guitar and from which he produced soft, buoyant melodies, mixed with floating singing in his local Hindi dialect. It totally captivated me and those around us. The music would build up, and then fall, rising again to some climactic bridge that washed over me as if all my cells were in alert and joyous with the sounds flooding through my body. When he finished, he would pause, just for a moment, as if he could see the falling flecks of matter floating in this magic moment, as if observing a tangible beauty. He nodded and smiled, chuckling to himself quietly, his eyes held it all, they held the story, the magic. He took a sip of his chai and lit a beedie.

*

Throughout all the lives I've encountered, not just on this trip but around the world, I've found that everyone wants the same thing. No matter your condition, race, class or religion, we all want the same; a good life, a healthy, prosperous life devoid of illness, loneliness and poverty. The more I rode the more I saw people and their extremely harsh ways of living, doing their best to survive, you and I are no different. Simple pleasures kept spirits high, cricket seemed a major pillar of happiness and a good cup of steaming hot chai seemed capable of solving most worldly issues.

Shadowing an Indian Poet

'We are here to laugh at the odds and live our lives so well that Death will tremble to take us.' - Charles Bukowski

Inside a dappled, pale blue house, a small lightless corridor leads to an opening, a room with a single chapped leather sofa, a barred window and beneath a leaning, dusty stretch of books of varying thickness and length. Some new and untouched, some with worn spines and folded corners from years of escapist pondering.

Three holes in a grey brick in the bathroom holds a grey light bulb, dusty from years of unuse, the others hold candles, match boxes and cigarette butts. A dark green shelf is built into the wall, the edges are black from years of searching fingers and greasy wrists, just like the marks in the hallway entrances at chest level, a few higher maybe from pauses for thought or as something to support the weight of a drunk Indian man whose heart has been filled with love from his homeland and an inquiring mind to make sense of it all in words and songs or transcribed into feeling through text.

The shelf in his bedroom is packed with more disjointed books, cooking oil, old sweet jars, a few glass trophies from his youth as a veracious writer, a small sculpture of Jesus and Mary in deep red and waxy cream, old aftershave bottles, incense sticks and the middle shelf had three dark patches of paint where the candles burnt for many years. A single deer horn balances on the top. Shakespeare, broken chess pieces, ripped spines and the cabalistic markings in Hindi sketched into the wall from delirium or maybe a lack of paper.

The moisture around the door frames spreads upwards, cobwebs lean in the frames and drift from the single roof fan, the wall markings in black ink and pencil permeate the walls.

We go for a drive in his car. He looks around giddily. He touches his heart with three fingers and a thumb as he drives past the church where his parents are buried. We light incense over their graves and surround them with candles. He prayed to them, his chin dropping onto his chest in sort of surrender, I put my arm around his shoulder and hold him for a moment.

We go to the murky backwaters surrounding his village. He wraps himself in a small hand towel and submerges into the hot waters somewhere in the rural stretch of land surrounding a tropical mesh of south India and its torrent of abundant, twisting, tropical forestry. The river stretches a 100 meters across and glides under a towering green corridor of palm, mango and jackfruit trees, and on the surface a thick islands of weeds and water lilies, three spiky flower heads bob on the surface in mustard yellow and marble white.

He submerged as if reciting a cleansing spiritual procedure of cleansing. A light and deep comfort overcame him after his reconnection with the water. Then he bursts into song in gorgeous Malayalam, head raised and slightly twisted. He sings to the water with his hands resting on the surface. He sings to his home. A man at one with his land, a real organism of that place, singing about it, from it, through it, into it.

Curiosity

"For it is said that humans are never satisfied, that you give them one thing and they want something more. And this is said in disparagement, whereas it is one of the greatest talents the species has." – John Steinbeck

'Just because you're curious doesn't mean that you're going to do something that's valid, but it does motivate you to go out and start looking and trying. We're all running curious, because in that lies the roots of creation' - North Face

When someone is curious there's often a level of ignorance involved. Being curious will lead you into unknown territory and provide a chance to explore something new, to learn and to grow in strength, experience and wisdom. I would tell people of my plans to cycle the length of India. Many would be buzzing with excitement for me and of course some would ask, 'Isn't it dangerous? Where will you sleep? What will you eat? I would always respond naively by remarking that I'll have a tent and I'll sleep anywhere that I could, on the side of the road or in field, that I have no idea where or what I'll eat but I'll eat whatever's available and deal with any danger in the moment. Some people looked at me with pity on their faces. There's a definitely a stubbornness in curiosity and likewise in whatever I do, if someone says something's too hard or too dangerous, it simply evokes in me a need to do it more, to prove them wrong and to prove myself that I *can* and not to be discouraged by other people's limitations.

Where there's negativity and doubtfulness around you in whatever you do, there's always an opportunity to turn it into positive challenge, a character building adventure to be attacked with confidence and enthusiasm.

The crux it seems of curiosity is that we are never satisfied, that once we get a taste for that exciting world outside the borders of our comfort and knowing, then we get hooked, and the feeling multiplies. Something greater that mere success is created, we shift our ignorance, we enrich our lazy minds, and feed on the milk self-discovery. I thought maybe this long, testing journey would satisfy the constant squeeze of curiosity I was experiencing, would simmer it down to a gentle bubble. In reality it did the opposite, now the heat has been turned up and waters of adventure-tinged inquiry are over spilling. Now, every global map I look at becomes a blueprint plot for an exciting new story, I imagine myself in far-fetched places across the globe, I point at random and think to myself what would it be like there, what stories would I have from cycling or walking through that country, or that mountain range or that incredibly long coastline. Extreme distances become playful thoughts to juggle with, what would it be like to walk the length of Russia, cycle the length of Africa or kayak around the Greenland? My whole attitude becomes stimulated with provocative quests and new experiences. Curiosity doesn't just

21

rest in the search for hardcore global exploration, it spills over into the mind of an individual. Curiosity is an attitude.

Youth

'You're too young to be panning memories Adam, you should be making new ones so that the mining will be richer when you come of age' – J. Steinbeck

We're always being told to make the most out of our youth. To do these things while you're young and you've got the time, to live life fully before the looming cloud of adulthood and responsibility kicks in. What does this mean, and surely, how can we know before it's too late? Everyone is different in this vision. Some see a two-month trip to South East Asia, all beach parties, vodka buckets and iconic landmarks as making the most of things, of *squeezing* in some travel, some freedom before they commit their life to something or someone else, 'you can carry on with life now, you've done it, now get back to work!'. Some people I have spoken to are already in the mindset, before they've even left their home country, that their short trip will be a mere tick on the 'To do' list, something to say that they've completed only to move on with the list, with their goal orientated life. Yes, they'll enjoy it and have fond memories, but this is where it will end. Of course, I aim to make the most out of my youth, but I *don't* do so in order to pinpoint the highlights of a life lived with the sort of freedom only associated with the chapters of my younger years, nor do I do it in a way to define who I am, It's simply part of the overall growth. There's no goal orientation with it, there's no overall objective, it's simply an embraced essence of life that I couldn't live in any other way, and with this comes the flooding satisfaction of the thing which I believe we must always listen to and trust the most; the heart. You should do what you believe in. Follow this feeling. Everything else is a lie.

But of course, some experiences take me deep into a youthful frenzy, a bubbling realisation of the budding life of a young man out in the winds of adventure.

Under the crimson curtain of dusk, shreds of clouds, like stretched cotton flared pink and then burnt out with the last minutes of blazing sunlight. Cycling through the hills of rural Rajasthan after a long, arduous day I pass bright gardens of lemon grass hemming slate stone houses enveloped in arching palm trees and tenanted by sleeping buffalo. I witness more pockets into worlds untouched (uninfected?) by modern civilization, scenes which haven't changed for thousands of years and probably won't change that soon either. As I cycled through these small callous patches of life either side of the sinuous track, children run out from the edges of the village waving and calling out in ecstatic, high pitched yells, chasing my back wheel with sticks and wide grins. I continued to ride into the terracotta evening as night falls. My headlamp broke so I use the shuddering light from my phone to lead the way, the track is unlit and I push on into the valley, into the increasing darkness of the hills now coated with a dark lilac haze, so lovely it looked scented.

I relished and beam a tired smile to myself in the image of what I was doing. I remember this clear sensation of insatiable pride, self-satisfaction, this oneness binding dreams and reality. And yes, it was shaping my youth, but defining it was the *novelty* of what I was doing and the strength that came knowing that I'd found something that fulfilled the thirst and that would forge incandescent rivers of adventure into the mountains of my eminent, promising future. Pulling hard on the handlebars, heart pounding, breathing heavy through cold night air, working my way towards a hilltop as the sky dips ink black and the moon hangs on my left shoulder like a pearl. I cycle on into the darkness, smiling all the way.

Several hours later I look out of a cheap motel window, it's too dark and I'm too tired to set up my tent. I have a bucket shower and then I boil some spaghetti with my stove on the balcony, which I then cover in ketchup. It's a cheap, but bland and pretty tasteless meal. Totally exhausted, I lean out of the window and listen to the sound of pigs scuffing through the waste below, it's is the only noise under the moon, that salmon-coloured moon, the only familiar object in this totally alien world.

*

Cycling the length of India is, quite frankly, silly. To others, on a practical basis, it's time wasting, unproductive, a lovely experience for sure, but ultimately an escape *away* from the 'real world', I see it as escaping *into* the real world, *towards* the real world.

It's a tedious, sweaty, enduring solo act, and I absolutely love it. Physically because of the extreme strains and challenges that I

25

get to put my strengthening body through, emotionally because of the heartache of leaving new friends and communities behind, only to dive into something new and further exposing myself to the next day's novelties.

My environment in England tells me to be focused on my career, on the important career building steps that will lead me to a good job and a good salary. I chose to cycle across India to trigger an adventurous life, to escape this delusion. I wanted more, I knew I couldn't call that life. It all seemed so systemised, so dry, and like there is, surely something bigger and better for ourselves.

Ultimately, I didn't cycle India for the sake of cycling that far, or even for cycling that particular country in that particular direction, I did it as a symbol of my escape, as a metaphor for how I want to live my life. A life full of colour, hardship, challenges and new experiences. A physical challenge, paired with self-discovery.

Discovery

'Sometimes your vision won't make sense to people because it's too big for small minds. Keep it to yourself and make it happen'

My legs burn and my wrists ache as I weave through the streets approaching a hillside town avoiding reckless lorry drivers, rapid school buses and the swarm of rickshaws. I rest on a giant slab of stone on the ridge of a hill overlooking a glorious multilayered town splayed across an impressive stretch of rolling pine-coated hills. The hard work is over for today as the sun dances over the town. This new exciting place is my reward for getting here.

Stacks of pastel coloured dwellings, British colonial architecture and decaying Tudor houses are all squinting in the gold of the setting sun. The sun mixes with the smog creating a hazy, amber hugh. The air is filled with the smell of waste and dust, traffic fumes and incense, steam and rusted metal and occasional pockets of fresh mountain air.

As I cycle through the town, I cut through a small tunnel and past a few backpackers thumbing through their Lonely Planet guide. I haven't seen a western face for a few weeks and it brings a whiff of familiarity to my senses. I have no idea what's in this town, I know nothing about it, have I stumbled across a tourist town, a place of rich cultural history, golden monuments, or famous architecture? This is the art of stumbling upon things, a subject that is found in the roots of touring, of riding to no real plan, into unknown territory. What's around this corner, what's in that mountain town dazzled in lights, what will I see in a month from now? That's all in the excitement to unfold.

As I roll further through the town a man shouts something and starts running towards me up an impossibly steep hill. He was a big guy, with a stocky neck, chubby face and a bouncing wheel of fat around his gut. 'Hotel Sir, you want room, cheap room?!'. Normally I'd continue cycling, aiming to find somewhere to put up my tent and agitated by their persistent hassling, but I appreciated the effort and told him to take a seat and catch his breath, still laughing at the image of him wobbling up the steep hill as sweat starting to roll down his face.

The hotel was a squalid, damp place with mould on the walls, dusty windows and used condoms in the bin. After throwing my bags down and then shouting at the manager to clean my room, I headed out into the town and admired the last golden hour of sunset and the colourful knot of people tumbling through the urban market. A warren of steep twisting steps wound down into the town passing limbless beggars and street merchants. One man dexterously tossed bread into a giant pair of square headed iron clamps that he heated over a gas stove to make toasties. His hands were rapid and his execution flawless. He cranked the clamps open with knife and threw the steaming, crispy bread into newspaper and showered it with chilli and cream.

Further down into the central market revealed a striving and electric market town. There was young, fresh eyed school kids, smart bank employers, labourers in torn vests lugging huge sacks of rice on their heads. There were hotel workers with waistcoats and slick back hair, neat finger width moustaches and polished shoes. There were men haltered to portable betting tables with straps of rope where people would come and place bets and drink chai.

For all of its tradition, age and location there are pockets of western life here, seemingly affluent, casual, technological, all squeezing its way out of a town on the side of a mountain high in the Himalayas. This is the evolving dichotomy of life across this developing country. It was my urge to travel to these remote, unassuming places to discover such wonderful sites where modern life is mixed in ancient pastime.

The sun went down long and red, glazing everything: my hand, the floor, the walls, the world. I shuddered in the sudden cold, with my fists deep in my jacket pockets. I watch monkeys climb up the mesh of electric cables draped between buildings and lamp posts, their babies clinging underneath to their stomach. They perch on the edges of rusty air-condition units, silhouetted by the sun and de-nit each other in the fading light.

I walk further through the town and into an open square, a sort of hill top promenade lined with lamps and scratching dogs, where a giant brass statue of Mahatma Gandhi stands overlooking the town and the pink ribbon left from the sunset hanging over the western hills. I pay a small boy ten rupees for a paper cup of chai that he pours from a big flask and I stand there in the cold eating hot popcorn from a nearby stand, looking up at the father of modern India.

Being out on the road allows me to cut a lot of the non-important information out of my life, allows me to filter through the crap. I'm reminded of the great spirit of a man whose life was a great devotion to cause. I was reminded of a man with a wholehearted purpose, a mission and a bold one at that. I'm definitely not going to change the world, and my purpose for being out here on this adventure is purely selfish, but I like to think that we share a little something in common in that respect. Around his neck hang fresh garlands of brightly coloured flowers, around mine a messy ring of popcorn crumbs.

Escape

'Life is too brief and too rich to tiptoe through half-heartedly, rather than galloping at it with whooping excitement and ambition. And so I explode in rage just in time. It's time to go prowling in the wilderness. It is time to live violently again. It is time to sort my life out.' - *Alastair Humphreys*

On top of the physical challenge and the craving accomplishment of a big, rich adventure is the fact that I just want to be somewhere new, on the other side of the planet, taking in breathtaking scenery and listening to beautiful music. I don't know who would want much more. To be taken out of daily routines, to feast upon new experiences, to jump out of your comfort zone and expose yourself to the rich world surrounding you. An ostensibly selfish act? Absolutely! Certainly, I love people, I'm a very gregarious individual and I do believe that happiness is best shared with others, but I need my time, my own lonely time out in the world to loose my feet and find them again, to measure my determination once a while, to test my resolve in the rawest way, with my own head, hands and feet.

Escaping can also be difficult. The get up and go attitude to life is a purely selfish one, one which moves forward irrespective of what's around them, it doesn't consider the people or the environment you might effect as a result. The crux of the modern day traveller. We leave behind worried families, friends and parents and they know there is a big risk involved. This is the result of you acting impulsively on your desires. The emotional debris you leave behind is part and parcel for a life of adventure. A life we all must embark on in our own different ways. However hard it maybe to leave the familiar world behind, no matter how ridiculous or stupid the idea it may seem, it's always an exchange for something much greater that what you left behind.

I've often hated myself for this, cursed at myself, and at my unquenchable thirst for escape. Why can't I just be happy leading a normal life, in comfort, just content with a job and safe living and predictability? Every story is of course subjective but in this story, as I hugged my parent's goodbye in Birmingham airport, an anchor of great weight pulled my heart down into my stomach as it knotted itself at the sudden realisation of what I was about to do and the worry I was about to put them through. I've always been very close to my parents. My face reddened and turned hot. It was my stubbornness, my careless life leaving the people who care for me in a dark cave of unknown. My father gave me a hug, I knew he was upset, his normally rugged manly hug turned into a soft embrace and dropped his neck into my shoulder, here, all at once came the sudden realisation that he wouldn't see me for over half a year, the hug itself felt like I was going away for much longer. He knew this trip included a lot more risk. I felt a tear roll down his cheek, I turn to look at him, but he shyly turned away covering his face and walked off without looking back, disappearing into the crowd of exciting looking families about to embarking on their summer holidays.

Through security, on the plane, heart still in my throat, we're hurtling down the runway, I look out the window towards the only familiar world I know passing rapidly by in the drizzling English winter, where my life up to now had existed, where my parents drive home and continue life without their son, where all knowledge of myself and my capabilities lie, from the arms of 'home'. I take a last deep breath, close my eyes, and lift up into the air. I'm on my way to India.

Reward

'As I make my slow pilgrimage through the world, a certain
sense of beautiful mystery seems to gather and grow'
-A.C. Benson

The sun dipped below the hilltops in the foothills of the
Himalayas, diffusing an orange glow throughout the valley.
Parallel to the road, a roaring, emerald river reflected the warm
tones of the burning sky above and like a giant green snake,
wound its way through the mountains with its scales
shimmering in the sun.
There was a wide stretch of white sand next to the river, I
pushed my bike down the bank and through the soft sand,
clearing the washed-up debris of old branches and patches of
sheep droppings and set up my little one-man tent in the sand.

The day was full of excitement and adrenalin and a flash of
activity. And now, as I sat in my open tent and reflected on my
first day's ride, observing the fading colours, the deep sound of
the river moving slowly on its long journey to the sea, the birds
hawking in the trees, a deep, all-consuming feeling of relaxation
settled over me.

Darkness fell quickly, and the valley filled with fresh, cold air, a
few bright stars started to shine above the black fissures of the
valley peaks surrounding me.

I took refuge in a small sheltered restaurant next to the river bank. Many truck drivers pulled over for a quick break and warmed their hands and feet over an open fire pitted against a few sheets of metal. This is very common across India in the winter, leaving winding mountain roads punctuated with flickers of amber light that delineate the low mountains from the cold, bruised sky. They appear in pockets and winding ribbons into impossible heights, just random points of light in the distance of an impossibly dark valley, tranquil yet riven by invisible ferocious rivers. A few thin, grey bands of cloud creeped in over the ridges, nudged closer together by a gentle breeze. The sound of crickets filled the valley walls.

I devoured plates of rice and steaming hot chai and fighting my sudden tiredness, accepted the invitation to join a small gathering of locals drinking whisky inside the restaurant kitchen. The interior was all bare-brick and chipboard, the corrugated steel sheets above us blushed amber from a wood fire. The kitchen was a blur of fast hands as staff slapped and stretched flowery dough into thin disks with their hands and tossed them onto steaming frying pans to make roti's. A few old sheep farmers smoking beedies observed me scrupulously, they had wiry eyebrows, a few remaining teeth and their faces were creased with deep ridges and lines. They sat crouched on a split wood bench with their hands joined in a type of week prayer and engaged in a rambling discussion eyeing me suspiciously. Their words rolled fluently, coming to sudden pauses, then trilling into short animated expressions, their heads loosely bobbing side to side playfully; that famous Indian head shake, ubiquitously used, rarely understood.

I was shattered. The adrenaline of the day had finally evaporated and I my body needed rest. My head was swimming ecstatically in the fleeting thoughts of the day's activity. Only three days ago I was in England. Now I was relishing in the flashbacks of snow peaked ridges, waterfalls, bridges coated in quivering prayer flags, a flash of portraits from the neighboring countries Nepal, china, India and Tibet. I sauntered back down to my tent down on the banks on the river and lay down with my back against a big rock and drank the last of my whisky from a small paper cup. The sky was a now a wash of clear, bright stars like dazzling shark's teeth splayed against a black curtain. I raised a cheers to the sky and retired to my tent to sleep next the deep roar of the river and the strong smell of sheep droppings.

On this long ride, there are some experiences that have rushed through me in skin prickling reverence for nature, wildlife, and the generosity of the human spirit. None of this would have been possible had it not been for a craving and lust for escape and the resulting exposure.

Himalaya

'There is a Truth, and it's on our side' - *Jose Gonzalez*

There's something very empowering about the grandeur of mountains. High in some small village surrounded by craggy snow kissed mountains and small huts piping out smoke from their chimneys, I set up camp for the night on the side of a hill next to sheets of hard snow. K2, the second highest mountain in the world, locally known as Nanda Devi is clearly visible from here, the eminent, sharp peak rising high into the air and penetrating the higher layer of clouds that glide smoothly over its summit. The west ridge is dressed in an orange glow from the sun and opposite is black and sinister looking. I walk down across the ridge and onto an ice-sheeted road to find somewhere to take photos of the sunset that was approaching fast. I pass some army barracks where the Indo-Tibetan army are playing a game of volleyball. The court is lined with rubber tires and a torn net is strung across the alpine floor propped up by two posts. They laugh and cheer and play enthusiastically, running around with their hands in the air and high-fiving their teammates whenever they scored a point. The referee sits on the corner and drinks what looks like liquor from a hip flask and smokes a cigarette. It's probably the most scenic place for a game I've ever seen.

I setup my camera on a tripod on a nearby ridge making a time-lapse of the sun dipping behind the mountains. I sit cross-legged on the cold, loose ground and breathe in the ice-cool mountain air. I breath in slowly, it fills my lungs, calms my heart rate. I sit in silence for a while.

I tell myself how thankful for this wonderful new day, my health, my life changing experience. How far flung out in the world I was, thriving in life with dirt under my fingernails and a fresh pack of biscuits in my pocket. My hands turn purple and pink from the bitter cold as I shove them in my jacket pockets and watch the azure sky change tone above me.

Deep shadows folded into the mountain side and giant, pink clouds of cotton wool stretch across the eastern sky. I feel like I'm sitting in some eminent kingdom of gods, their snowy crowns blazing all around me.

This is why I came out here. To feel sublime amongst such epic nature and to tune into the insignificance of those things which can burden us on the surface, money, image, fame, success. To realise our mortality and impermanence in the face of these ancient mountains which have lived a thousand years before me and will live a thousand years after I have left. I travel for these perspective enhancing moments. I feel lucky and inspired by being in certain places that cultivate and reconnect my sense of wonder with the world.

I walk back absolutely freezing despite all the clothes I have; fleece, two jumpers, down jacket, leg warmers, long johns, and walking trousers. I collect some firewood on the way back to my tent, scratching and pricking my fingers as I snap branches off thorny and tough alpine bushes. I dump it all next to my tent hoping to light it and keep warm later.

The people are so nice to me up here, one man who runs a small guesthouse for skiers welcomes me in where I'm given free tea and dinner, provided that I help make it. I spend some time cutting peppers and rolling out chapatis and frying them on a hob. He also has a cabernet full of alcohol and I buy a small bottle of rum off him. After the dinner I thank my host and walk back to my tent down on the ridge with a bottle of rum stuffed in my pocket. I light the firewood, taking off my shoes and socks to warm my freezing feet and drink my rum in silence under a brilliant, black sky animated with a million stars.

*

I unzip my tent the following morning to a blazing sun piercing through the jagged peak of the mountains surrounding me. Long, amber rays fill the valley, illuminating the cold earth and all the small dwellings that had kept their fire going through the night, their chimneys still billowing out smoke in a blue haze. I packed up all my gear, returned the two thick blankets that I borrowed from the guesthouse and headed off down the endless, sinuous switchbacks that were draped across the mountain. The roads were steep and icy, and the air was bitterly cold. I wore all the clothes I slept in and my gloves did nothing to prevent the harsh wind biting at my fingers as I plummeted down the mountain roads. Only a handful of minutes had passed when I approached a tight bend in the road and braked accordingly, I leaned tight into the apex of the road and saw what I thought was a small river of water running across the road surface from a little stream, but as I got closer and merely six feet away from it I recognised the shiny, marble type texture of black ice, it was too late at this point, my front wheel hit the surface smoothly but as soon as the back wheel and all its weight hit the ice the whole bike collapsed underneath me throwing me clean off and scraping along the floor. I swore a lot, staggered to the side of the road and assessed the damage. My thigh and knee were badly grazed, and a little stream of blood rolled down my shin, my right elbow which broke the majority of the fall was also cut, tearing straight through two layers of my thick down jacket and hoodie. I was shaking with the adrenaline, cold, and clutching my arm in pain. I took a minute to rest on the side of the road. I cleaned and bandaged my knee, stuffed as much as the padding back into my down jacket as I could and wrapped it up tightly in gaffer tape. I then continued with the long descent, a little slower and cautiously around the sweeping bends as I worked my way further and further down through the mountains, avoiding roaming cattle all the way, sweeping through the beautiful mountains of the glowing Himalayas.

A Lesson in Regret

'Sometimes you have to go ahead and do the most important things, the things you believe in, and not wait until years later, when you say, "I wish I had gone, done, kissed..." '

I make a rare pit stop at one of the more luxurious restaurants off the highway that runs through northern India's desert state of Rajasthan. Tour companies bring their guests here for lunch breaks as they rush between their destinations in their air-conditioned taxi's. An iron trellis coated in beautiful flowers and weeds opens up to into a lush garden circumvented with terracotta walls and carvings on their pillars. It had an expensive gift shop at the front and verdant gardens ringed with palm trees attended by straight-backed staff, clean shaven and dressed in pristine white jackets. I sat down and ordered the cheapest thing on the menu.

A mini bus pulled up in the parking area. I got used to easily identifying which vehicles carried tourists, normally white Hyundai's with polished wheel hubs.

Several English people folded out and walked into the gardens, they sat on the table next to me. They all wore clean, colorful clothing with beautiful floral shirts and white shorts. They drank cold beer, ate vast amounts of food and talked excitedly about their next destination, one of them was repeatedly informing the others from a guide book. Their driver sipped chai quietly on a separate table.

My shirt was creased and thick with dust off the road and rings of encrusted sweat spread under my pits and down my back in rivulets. I stunk!

After finishing my meal and complaining to the waiter about the price of my coke, which was written on the bottle and yet charged double, I headed over to chat to them, I felt compelled, partly through curiosity, partly through excited ego. There's definitely an ego in big adventures, no matter how humble one may seem, every mountain climber, every long-distance explorer, carries with them a bold ego of personal endeavour and psychological challenge which in turn drives them to pursue such big dreams and actively participate in them.

One of them men was drilling me with enthusiastic questions, he was in his late forties with a thick Newcastle accent, he had a shaved head and taught wrinkles webbed around his fresh eyes. He spoke softly and upbeat, but I sensed an inner frustration deep down in the nuances of his voice that sunk somewhere deep in my memory. He asked me why I was doing it, how this was shaping up my life so far, where's next and a few other enthusiastic stabs in interest. There was a moment of silence. I saw the light in his eyes. Eye to eye. He let out a sigh and a shake of his head. The clean shirt and sandals seemed suddenly lost on him, like he suddenly realised what his essence of travel *could* have been. The tone of regret, one of the saddest sounds. He was suddenly a reflection of the older me that wished he had done something like that when he was younger. I observed a sense of nostalgic regret, the young zealous explorer inside of him, squeezed out by his adult life, the full-time job, the family, the other commitments. The painfully poignant look in his childlike eyes reminded me of my journey and the grand importance what I was doing with my time. I convinced myself that I wouldn't get to a stage in life where I regretted the things that I could have done, but didn't, instead I would make incredible adventures, and pursue this theme tirelessly and relentlessly for as long as I could. All mindful, and heartfelt decisions have wonderful repercussions. This meeting would prove to be one of the most important in this long, endless journey.

I said goodbye and pushed off again into a whirling headwind reuniting with my sore legs and aching wrists on a highway shared by lorry's, mopeds and camels pulling carts of people that waved as I cycled past. They pass in their taxi moments later, waving out of the back of the window and taking photos. It's nice to think I'm in their life now, and they're in mine. Maybe a blurry photo of me exists in their photo album, small against the backdrop of the vast, flat landscape, dust kicking over me and huge grimace on my face as I wave them onto the rest of their journey.

*

As I lie down in my tent later that evening, I think again of the group of English people I met earlier, as they rush from one city to another, missing out on the intricate beauty I felt so lucky to be experiencing. I think the world is a place to roam slowly, piece by piece, moment by moment, if you travel quickly, you miss out on the real rhythm of a place as it unfolds.

Identity

'And who in his right mind has not probed the black water?' J. Steinbeck

'Let yourself be silently drawn by the stronger pull of what you really love' - Rumi

The open road again. As I left Rishikesh for the second time, up in the foothills of the Himalayas, a huge sense of removal and loss was balanced with a very new feeling, I felt for the first time that I was becoming a tourer. I was no longer simply jumping from place to place, but weaving places and stories together through the act of riding my bike. It became one continuous vision, a constant stream of memorable images and experiences that soften and made malleable my appetite and fierce tenderness for life. I felt like someone else. New Jack, travelling Jack. Bushy bearded with wild strawy hair, actually used to the melee and chaos and dust and music and dangerous drivers and a thousand strange glares. More importantly I left with a heavy heart, filled to bursting already with people and experiences. I rode out into the endless stretches of road, back out into solitude, up mountain passes, across huge stretches of barren land, all in a state of consciousness, in tune with a certain *feeling* that I was feeding, all that existed was me, my bike and the changing landscape - and all obstacles and challenges were merely things to be endured and savoured.

*

I'm a figure unconsumed and undetermined by social gain, undefined by ideals, I give but a taste of who I've become and what I've done to the outside world. This journey is personal, inward, justified by personal benefit, not of the interest of others. I cycle a lot through this land but I also walk. I walk in the shadows of voiceless Indian towns, past smoke smudged niches dripping with marble wax, beneath the cover of palm trees, under rusting steel shelters, amongst cobwebs and fresh flowing mountain rivers, remnants in whispers and short tongue in lost and confused towns where the russet dust kicks up and the bananas ripen red, the yellow mustard fields stretch out into endless evanescence and no one knows who I am. But I was there, that was me, pedaling hard with dust in my eyes and darkened eyelids, skin parched dark brown from months under the sun, a fruit fly stuck to my sweaty forehead, several in a greasy mane of hair grown thick and knotted on the stifling head of an idealist twenty three year old out on the road. That was me, I'd never felt so alive. Cycling Jack. Or in fact, the knowledge of who I was not anymore, someone different, something forged, shaped differently. I was no longer who I thought I was, as if cycled away from the fictional identity that I was acting out before. I felt fresh, reborn, clear of my intentions, of my simple, liberating purpose.

*

I was born in England, but India fills me with a sense of joy and an element of belonging. I'd part ascribed myself a new nationality, not one I was born into but once that I was attracted to, one that made me dream. I've ventured further through its body than my home country and has offered me more wild experiences than anywhere before. How can I not feel some deeper weighted identity with it?

Amongst the Chaos

'To go and actually make a choice and to gain some
awareness of who you are, why you are what you are is
priceless'

India is a place of paradox, of contradiction, a place of
commerce and spirituality, a dichotomy of chaos and
tranquility. I'm in a small yet busy town in the northern crease
of the Himalayas, the emerald river Ganga runs majestically
past the hard knees of many towns and it's devotees. The
constant buzz of traffic and squawkers are interrupted with
pockets of meditative, hypnotic sounds spilling from the hearts
of surrounding temples and ashrams, sacred practices kept alive
in these mountains. There are real gurus smoking hash among
the Ganga here.

I rest my bike against a tree and down onto the sandy banks of
the river. People around seem deep and sentient. As the evening
breaks people migrate from the narrow streets down onto the
shore for that final golden, sacred hour. They sit and play
music, meditate, give out prayers, contemplate.

To sit alone beside the Ganga in twilight is to experience
undisturbed tranquility, a very powerful place and time to be
alone. The river flows as it has done for thousands of years and
like it will for thousands more when I have gone. Like many
rivers around the world the movement continues with or

without me. The transient beauty inspires my sense of time and space, it brings me into appreciation of the joy and power of now and of where I am in the world in a serene and alert way. I contemplate where I am in the world and how I got here. What a rich, beautiful opportunity taken with both hands, I feel so grateful to be all the way out here!

I sat in the sun in a languid doze, folded my legs underneath me, they're tight and strong from the day's ride. I dive into thought, a deep reflection helped by the flow of the river. I think about the journey so far, the amazing challenge, the daily novelties, the new-found enthusiasm for my incredible life on the road. I turn to see monkeys jumping between mossy arms of pine trees. The first wave of thoughts already wound around the corner of the river, lost forever taking with it soil, debris and ash and along with it, hopes, dreams and gratefulness. Everyone has their spot and time to sit and think on the banks of the Ganga, India's holiest river, where millions of prayers are dashed out to it everyday, feeding the hearts and mouths of so many millions who devote and depend upon it.

Just like the pace of India, my journey can often be quick, flashing past intricate sections of life, a thousand stories and lives pass by every day; a face behind the trees, a man in tattered suit and hat under a palm, a group of children crossing a bridge holding hands.

All these details and wonderful intricacies of life in India surround me everyday, surrounded by so much noise and activity, beautiful silences in the whirling chaos of India.

They are people in their moment, their own little fragile worlds. I am most fond of these moments, they provide the most wonderful, short lived experience of the real people and moments of the journey, caught in the quick flash of the eye. Just two individuals passing through two different lives, each one so vastly different from the last, our circumstances so different, our cultures so different, our attempts at life, so vastly different.

I filter down through the rough, winding track of a cold forest, and into an old mining town where a few small bazaars selling only chai, omelettes and cigarettes are sitting in the constant shadow of the valley.

From above a busy bridge I look over and down on to the banks of a river, it's flanked by a surface of ragged rocks on one side and dense, over spilling forest on the other. A woman in a bright orange lungi walks down the steps to the river and lights a candle in a dried coconut husk, there's a guru smoking in the sun perched on the crumbling lip of a temple balcony. Across the river an old paunch-bellied man with his worn body is praying in the water, lifting his hand in the air and bringing them back down to his heart. All the while, rattling rickshaws, choking lorries and loud buses steam over the bridge and pass by noisily and relentlessly.

Diggers and men with chainsaws smack and saw and rip through metal, stone and wood in a nearby quarry. Life here, even in the most remote of places is industrious, loud and dirty. A great pall of black smoke rises from the construction area and drifts up and into the arms of the tree-armoured cliffs surrounding me. India is so alive and I feel grateful to see it's ever changing face, and the worldly different lives and intricacies that live within its ancient lands.

Later on that day, while descending rapidly through a stretch of forest in the northern slopes of Himachal Pradesh, I tie together beautiful, smooth sweeping s-bends and lean into the corners, feeling the weight of the bike shift underneath me seamlessly. The sun streaks through the tree line and warms the side of my face, giving it a warm glow. I stop for a moment and enjoy the fingers of amber light breaking through the trees. The trunks are covered with soft moss and alive with the nesting habits of small birds.
I see a movement across the path. An adolescent girl is combing her hair on the balcony of a small, stony house on the side of the road. Her back arched slightly, head titled to the side as she brings the mass of wet, black hair into a knot. It's a beautiful site. The wall behind her is turquoise and peeling like old stucco, smudged black with smoke and grease like an old Cuban fresco.

Behind the chaos, the mess and the struggle, India is a place full of beauty, and cycling allows me to capture these beautiful moments as they unfold naturally.

Times of Day

'In the midst of change we often discover wings that we never knew we had' - *Ekaterina Walter*

Morning

I like how my fingers can wake up and fumble around new textures and surfaces every day. One day it could be the inside canvas of my tent, the next, a soft pillow, soil, beautifully carved art nouveau bed heads, metal, rough carpet, sandy wood.

I awake to the peachy rose of dawn, hearing the hum of trucks and rickshaws like a great migration of roving cattle moving swiftly over the brick red earth, kicking up the hot desert sand, shrouding trees in a misty glow. That classic Indian theme tune against the first light of sun would be my opening soundtrack almost everyday. It's a sound and a feeling I miss when I'm back home, that chaotic, bustling world outside the thin walls of my tent, the world alive, a thousand two stroke wildebeest and the roaring shred of bulging tires, horns, distorted music, 'chai, chai, chai' and the incessant bell-ringing of a man selling roasted monkey nuts from his cart on the side of the road.

The small, remote towns in the mountains of the Himalayas are mornings to be savoured, they arouse every waking sensation with the lung-satisfying flood of fresh mountain air, the sweet smell of glacial water and the sight of layers of sun moving slowly up the rock-face and through into the narrow streets where men start lighting their kerosene burners and warming their hands over the fire.

The world is fresh, and the air is clear, mixed continuously with the smells of fresh vegetables, chai and the slight hint of foul, decaying waste.

I walk across the street from my small guest house to a small chai stall, perched on the steep slope of a hill, host to a few hundred small dwellings and food markets stacked on top of each other, the village in its entirety lives on one long bend in the road with a roaring glacial river running below it; the bus station, fruit market, sweet shop, stationery shop, tailors and newsagent, all clustered together in the smog of the morning, and the lonely track, *my* lonely track, leading up and away through the high valley in the distance. I sit there in silence and drink my tea and a few omelette sandwiches, breathing out warm vapour in the freezing air, watching pigs scuff through piles of rubbish below. I see groups of children stepping out of their houses wrapped in scarves and hats with their mothers on the way to school, I wave at them and they wave back in excitement.

My legs are cold, it's time to start the day, I drink one more cup of steaming hot tea and jump onto my bike. It feels incredibly heavy, but my legs feel strong and my bowels feel strangely at ease, I push on and up the steep track, it's so hard to get going, the incline is steep and the track is bumpy, I want to stop after only ten minutes but I grind on regardless and look down onto the town, getting smaller and shrinking further and further away from the lap of the cold mountain.

Daytime

Dark, muscular women carrying mountains of wood on their heads walk with downcast eyes along blisteringly hot roads. Their faces are barely visible under their saris and they turn to look at me as I cycle past. Their pink, spiral motif saris revealing small slices of their waists that ripples with the weight. Small children shadow them dragging bundles of sticks along the floor.

On either side of the road I see the real India. There are small thatched dwellings with pink walls cracked from the heat, storks of sugar cane being pressed through mangles, goats tied by the neck to mounds of bricks, donkeys scratching their heads on ploughs, women sculpting cow dung into flat circular disks and laying them down in rows on the muddy courtyards. There are pools of stagnant water, waste and garbage festering on the roadside and slender white egrets perch nonchalantly on the rough hind of buffalo, nose ringed and neck deep in water pools, chewing methodically in the sun.
As I cycled past bystanders they stopped and stared in amazement. Some open mouthed and baffled, some shout something inconceivable and point. But it was the children who went crazy at the sight of me pedaling through their town.

Through almost every village they would run or turn round on the bicycles and chase me, screaming and laughing giddily, 'hello sir, hello, hello, hello, how are youuuuu?!' continuing to chase until their legs can go no further. I would pass a school and the children would be having an outside class and they would see me over the wall outlining their playground, it would only take one to turn and point and the whole class would run up and spill onto the road waving and shouting. This is a routine experience for me but it's nice to know that I'm a rare experience in their day, something to remember, that special day the pink, sunburnt Englishman cycled passed their school.

I alleviate some back pain by resting my palms in the centre of the handlebars, (there's only three positions which I'm restricted to for six months) I view my surroundings from a slightly altered angle, below average eye level and look out into the open mist of palm groves and mustard fields that stretch on as far as the eye can see. Occasionally I can make out the small roaming, bent-back figures of farmers deep amongst the shrub, they have no idea that I'm passing through their remote town unaccustomed to any foreign appearance. I enjoy my secret passage through this sometimes quiet land.

The air is perfumed with a thousand different smells. Every few kilometers brings with it new intoxicating smells. Roasted sugar cane (it has a strikingly similar smell to Heinz tomato soup) the hind and dust of cattle, goats, horse, pig, buffalo, camels, burning wood, rusting metal, diesel fumes, coal smoke and beedies. I breathe in India and her immense fragrant body.

Night

In a remote part of northeast India, near the borders of Tibet, a small town is scattered across either side of a river.
The dwellings are black and smudged, and I see people washing in the river as the last fingers of sunset fall through the valley in a final glistening blaze. The wind starts to blow down from the hills and a steady chill sees more people wrapping up in scarves and blankets, hats get forced on children and groups of men sit closer to the kerosene cookers.

The last of the daylight is finally washed away and a darkness takes over beneath a sickle moon. The streets hawkers are now in full force as crowds of people gather around sipping on steaming chai and eating bags of popcorn. Old women waft coals, roasting corn on metal gridded trays against brick walls where cows continue to chew their way through the piles of rubbish on the street.
Hands are rubbed together and people shout down for an order of chai from their terraces. In front of a lucid coloured sweet shop, a spindly armed man pipes a runny liquid into a giant simmering pot of oil, sieving them out seconds later revealing sticky jalebi's, ropy orange sweets shaped like pretzels. They go straight into rolled newsprint and into the hands of hungry, excited children.

India at night has its own wild rhythm. The river runs black and rips its way through the valley floor. I walk out from a typically squalid guest house and walk through the dim lit street and across a bridge in my socks and flipflops, avoiding narrowly piles of rubbish, shit and pigs rusting through the dirt. I feel the chill of hundreds of eyes on me as I walk. The river roars underneath and a cold chill drifts off its surface. Far away music blasts across the valley, chanting, beating drums, squalling trumpets, the only other sounds are the rush of the river and metal workers working late into the night.

Several little concrete shelters dotted throughout the higher streets overlook the town like pillboxes. Inside, the floors are covered with burnt incense, graffiti scrawled across the walls with charcoal, 'I love you' and 'love and peace' were proclaimed on the ceiling.

These simple encounters are big rewards after a hard day hauling a bike up endless mountains. I walk back to the guest house, savouring every step, wanting it to last, wanting to stay awake and soak it all in more but I don't, I rest and fall into a deep sleep.

Hospitality

'If you are not willing to risk the unusual, you have to settle for the ordinary' - *Jim Rohn*

While descending down a steep mountain track, something snaps with a sudden metallic *clang* and the bike collapses underneath me, I'm thrown head first over the handlebars and slammed down onto my back, winded and struggling for breath. I get up slowly and assess any damage by moving my arms and legs, feeling that my teeth are still all there and there's no blood coming from anywhere. I heave my bike up off the floor and see that the front pannier rack snapped, throwing nuts and bolts across the path and down into the forest shrubbery. It turns dark quickly and it takes me an hour to find all the small pieces of metal, unload all the bags and slowly piece everything back together with a head torch. It's only my second night and i'm absolutely thrilled to be tracing through some dark woods, led by a small light and to the sound of my bags rattling over the stones and loose gravel. This is what I came for. Moments of nervousness arrive, it's dark, I've got no food, where will I put up my tent? But all these feelings are overshot by the excitement of it all and I start to see bright stars moving between the high tips of the pine trees above.

A light appears through trees and I approach a man closing down his small wooden shop. He's small and chubby with wiry eyebrows and kind, hazel eyes. I ask him if there is a safe place to camp and he replies excitedly that there is a guesthouse available nearby and he will take me there.

Tired, in pain and relieved, I follow the waddling man swinging a bulky LED torch to light the way. We walk up a steep track, through a field, across a small trail that falls steeply away to tall grass and reeds, through several wooden gates, a cluster of goats, up several stone steps and to a dimly lit wooden dwelling perched on a floor of concrete that is unmistakably his own house. The man shouts something and two young children rush out the house and are shocked to find their father with a pink, dishevelled looking foreigner with muck and oil on his face pushing a bike through their front garden, we all greet with giddy smiles and go inside. Inside the house his wife is preparing an array of food, fresh roti, curried veg, brown rice and sour yogurt.

This family is obviously poor, they only have a few cooking utensils and I'm amazed at how much food she has made with so little. A metal chimney runs from the gas cooker straight through the centre of the small room making it incredibly cosy and warm. I'm encouraged to take off my shoes and sit on one of the matted carpets next to the food and I'm handed a fresh glass of water. Naturally, I look for the cutlery but I think better than to ask, the children stare as I struggle to wolf down handfuls of steaming curry as it drips through my fingers and onto my lap. They offer me more and more and I happily comply, devouring as much food as I could until at last I slipped into a deep food slumber and nearly fall asleep on the warm floor.

We all clean our teeth together, a worldwide routine that defies country and class, only *we* do it in the darkness of night under a blanket of stars and spit into the long reeds of grass below, chuckling with the children at our simple routine. I sleep wonderfully through the night and I'm awoken to the sound of cockerels and sickles thrashing corn in the fields. A feast of a breakfast is awaiting me.

*

Something I learnt very quickly in India is that a 'Hotel' doesn't always mean a hotel in the conventional sense of accommodation. At the end of a piping hot, 120 Kilometer ride through central Rajasthan, I was relieved when I saw a 'Hotel' sign arched over a beautiful, ivory cladded gateway and welcoming smiles at the driveway entrance. After collapsing onto a plastic chair, the legs sewn together with thin rope, I flicked off my sweaty shoes, threw the burning socks on the cool, tiled floor and indicated my thirst for a chai as I slouched back and enjoyed the shade from the tarpaulin sheet above me. The sun was still burning down in its last few hours, my thighs were burnt at the line of my shorts and my calves were tight and exhausted so I was a little deflated when he replied quite plainly, 'sorry sorry, here no room, here only restaurant', bobbing his head side to side as he spoke.
After talking to the owner for some considerable time about where I had come from and where I was going, by this point his

entire family had come out to see me, he didn't hesitate to offer me a place in his house for the night.

Later that evening after a hot shower and a colourfully paletted tray of food that could've easily fed five men, he invited into a nearby town on his motorbike. We zoomed through the night down the highway through the smells of sand and tarmac and into the rumbling cacophony of horns, bikes, rickshaws and pedestrians, I spot a few young boys tug on the arm of their friend in excitement and point at the funny looking white boy on the back of a locals bike with his feet swinging with the rapid swerve of the bike.

I'm taken to an impressive looking temple and sit down at the back of the room where around two hundred people, men, women, entire families are sat on a swirling vibrant rug watching a film on a giant projector. The film is in Hindi of course with no English subtitles but the moral messages of family, education, friendship and honesty are clear. It's great to tap into pockets of people's lives and witness their different ways of teaching and developing their own communities, if only for a day. After the film and a rapturous round of applause, two orange swathed gurus are introduced into the room and take to their chairs on a stage festooned with flowers and golden sculptures of deities I had never seen before. A highly energetic man then starts rambling into a microphone from the front of the hall. My new friend looks at me giddily and persuades me to write my name and home city on a napkin. Then, his rapid and twisting Indian discourse is punctuated with 'English man from the city of 'Burn-mingham'. The hall burst into applause, my face reddened and I'm told to stand up in front and come to the stage to introduce myself. As I approach, the gurus bless me and halter me with garlands of orange flowers around my neck. I say a few nervous words down the microphone, a lot of their faces are stunned and smiling as I speak, and then I thank them kindly for their warm welcome and leave to another round of applause. The ceremony was followed by yet more great hospitality as they took me down to the open room beneath the temple where giant pots of stewing curry were being stirred by women with what looked like wooden awes. They sat me down and filled my plate up with mounds of rice, Dahl, curry and curd. We struggled to leave on the bike afterwards because of the queue of people wanting to shake my hands, but we finally made it away and back out into the sandy winds of the night.

The following day after refusing to only let me eat half a portion of breakfast, he takes me in his car with his wife to visit some other temples and to visit a local Osho ashram centre. He prepares one more cup of tea and a plate of biscuits before I'm finally ready to go at nearly midday, I hug him and his family, try to offer him money which he strongly refuses, take a picture and continue my lonely way towards Mumbai touched and humbled by the beauty of strangers which are in abundance across this amazing country.

Happiness

'There is an ecstasy which marks the summit of life...this ecstasy comes when one is most alive, and it comes as a complete forgetfulness that one is alive' - Jack London

I cycle the dim, low hanging pathway through the forest towards the charming, ethereal sounds of bells and rhythmic clapping in the distance. I'm in Rishikesh, a place set aside in ancient time, wearing a blanket of majestic song, pitched in a high, major key that falls over hippies and vagabonds, a sacred place that holds many prayers and callings and longing from its past and present inhabitants.

The sun sets behind the canopy and shards of light find their way through the tree line casting red and orange light onto the draggled hind of cattle chewing through the garbage piles on the side of the road. I'm in my down jacket and wrapped in a warm shawl, my arm is still patched up with gaffa tape from a crash I had in the mountains.

I find the source of the sound; a gathering of around three hundred devotees in the grounds of a hindu temple, sitting on the sloping steps by the edge of the river Ganga. Taking off my shoes and socks to stand on the cold marble at the top of the steps, I'm suddenly drowned in a beautiful choir of voices. A group school children wrapped in bright orange lungis sit in the centre and sing with their eyes closed. They surround a well, decorated with flowers, candles and incense spiralling up in tendrils of smoke. The entire crowd starts chanting 'Hare

Krishna' mantras, allowing rich, sonorous melodies to rise with the distorted tones a great bearded man bellowing through a microphone. There were men walking around circulating brass horns holding candles as people swayed their heads and bowed with the music, bringing their hands into their chests with unwavering smiles.

I stood there alone in the cold gentle breeze, the night pulled its curtain over the mountains which was now dark as slate and lined with the kiss of the moon. I felt incredibly blessed, not at the direction that life had taken me, but the direction that *I* took with my life, the action that *I* had taken which resulted in witnessing this experience. I brought my hands together and looked up and around in awe of this place and let the heartwarming mantras fall over me as I beamed a smile across the whole scene. I caught a glimpse of a western women looking at me from across the colourful knot of people in the crowd, she saw me beaming that incredible smile in the cold and she smiled back. I wonder what she thinks of me. What she thinks I'm doing here. I turn that question then to myself and realise straight away the significance of my happiness. I was simply connected to the understanding of my desires, aligning with my dreams and feeling incredibly joyful for this wonderful, random encounter that was a result of my travels on two wheels. Any change in the mode of transport, of pace, would of ultimately led me somewhere very different. And in that point this moment was all mine, I had made it, it was unique to my life.

This was one of the primary moments of pure joy.

I started to fall in love with my life. Never had I been so happy with where I was and what I was doing and happy with myself for making this decision. This was my way.

The open chanting and singing on the river steps continued throughout the night, and stayed with me to this day, as did that river, a deep orange glow moving slowly through the background, on a long, winding journey.

Spirit

'And when, on the cold still nights, he pointed his nose at a star and howled long and wolf like, it was his ancestors, dead and dust, pointing nose at star and howling down through centuries and through him' - Jack London

Although my days have a routine, the experiences along the way are far from predictable, far from ordinary. It's exciting and nerve-racking, at times disappointing and shocking, at times delightful and bewildering. Moving through life this way is feast for the open mind and a satisfying squeeze for the soul of spontaneity. I love waking up and not knowing what I'll encounter and I especially love cycling straight into the warm path of a setting sun without knowing where I'll sleep that night; a garden or a ditch under palm trees, a locals house or a cheap motel.

Somewhere high in the foothills of the Himalayas, the cold gravel summit of a mountain pass provides a perfect place to set up camp for the night. It's bitterly cold and below the ridge is a thick forest of evergreen trees, the last nuggets of sunlight clinging in their boughs. The sky is a sheet of pink, orange and blue melting into each other like a watercolor in a child's sketchbook.

A single concrete shelter with a goat tied up outside is the only shelter around, several old farmers are mixing rice in a deep copper cooking pot over a wood fire. Deep shadows fall over their bodies, the wall behind is a black wash with ash from the hundreds of fires. They don't speak a word of English, but I help to stir the rice as we continue to communicate through sign language. The moon rises, the stars reveal themselves. The night is icy black. I stumble outside for some fresh air my legs are tight and sore from the day's ride. I climb to the top of nearby ridge and listening to 'Big Hard Sun' by Eddie Vedder, the epic theme tune to the soulful film 'Into the Wild', a song wrapped in audacious veils of adventure synonymous with that rich heart of Christopher Mccandless. I started to scream at the stars. I felt a gigantic rhythm beating within me, so wild and happy amongst such epic nature. I have traveled far, pushed myself further than ever, my skin and bones, my head and my heart are right here, in this far away crease in the surrounding Himalayas on a clear cold night, the warmth from the fire slowly fading down from my fingers and then out of my palm.

On my return to the shelter I notice that the goat is no longer there. Inside now holds a different stench and I notice fatty clumps of meat simmering in the pot. A punchy man in a fur coat thrusts an offering of what looks like scrunched up newspaper in my hand, it's blotchy and heavy. I open it to find the goats heart. For the rest of the night the men continue to regale me with gestural stories, music and lavish amounts of goat stew smothered in chili and pepper. The heart was tough and bitter.

*

The first swells of morning light break the horizon and start to warm the forests below. The changing light falls on my tent and melts the ice that veiled it during the night. I open the zip, inhaling the first fresh breath of the day, the smell of pine and glacial water fills my lungs. I'm tired. I'm happy. The dirt and grime of last night's meat clings under my fingernails, hair straw dry, thick with ash and the scent of smoke from the fire. My face is patchy and dry until a boiled water wash from the copper cooking pot. As I start to collapse my tent and load my bike I notice the goatskin, hung out in ribbons from a tree for it to dry in the early alpine sun.

Place

'I felt absolutely free....a mixture of ignorance and a loose, 'what the hell' kind of confidence that comes to a man when the wind picks up and he begins to move in a hard straight line towards an unknown horizon' - Hunter. S. Thompson

Making it to the centre of a city or to some famous landmark, to the beach or to a hostel with tables studded with beers and attractive european girls was, of course, fun but it was not at the centre of my purpose on this journey, nor was it where I found the purest forms of delight, discovery or amusement on this adventure.

What was highly amusing however, was the day I rode into a hostel in Agra, the famous home to India's iconic Taj Mahal. I had just spent around a week traversing a long, hot splay of land from a mountainous state further north. The road was tough and dirty, almost always covered in clouds of dust kicked up from passing traffic and the smoke billowing out from brick factories and sugar cane roasters. By the time I arrived at the hostel I hadn't showered in five days. I cycled down the entrance path and through the garden where several young travellers were lounging in giant bean bags. They were all fresh faced, cleanly shaven and leafing through their guide books. My face was patchy with dirt, I had oil all over my hands and wrists, my hoodie looked moth-bitten and covered in a combination of dust, oil, sweat and droppings of greasy food. I went a collected a beer from the bar and collapsed onto the floor next to them, popping the bottle with my teeth and greeted them with a booming 'Hey, what's up guys!'. The bewildering look on their face indicated their interest but also that their sense of smell was perfectly sensitive.

*

I enjoy more the back streets in some dishevel old town, where weak lamps fall over rickety cobbles and leave shadows in the cracks. I prefer the dirt and stone, the dust, mess and stench, the things that tell me I am in real India, a thousand miles away from home, this is what I came for. I have no real idea where I am, somewhere deep in the lower creases of the Himalayas, in a small cobbled town where the sound of distorted prayers from a nearby temple fills the streets and the rusting houses are stacked incredulously on top of each other in some impossible fashion. I drink a beer on a cold stone outside a tailor shop. I'm staying in his spare room above the shop. It's nearly midnight yet the two men continue to thread like they did all day only now they wear scarves and a bottle of dusty rum sits on the table between them, they smile and offer me a small glass. On the floor next to me, a gaunt dog scratches incessantly at its skin, I feel kind of sorry and empathetic for it, lying there in its dirty bed of waste and brick, but then it shakes off and, moves down the road wagging its tail seemingly happy and nonchalant, this makes me smile. And then *BOOM!*, children set off fireworks in the street out of nowhere and cave in with laughter at the sight of me jumping out of my skin with shock. They continue to spark fire crackers through the streets, just the thudding reverberations off the fireworks and their excited screams now fill the empty streets in the darkness.

*

The day is burning hot, the sun is high now and pounding down on my head. A beautiful looking temple catches my attention in the distance. I pass a spindly legged man selling popcorn from his tiny shack on the side of the road and through the guarded gates into the grounds of a beautiful towering ashram. It's shady and slightly cooler inside and I enjoy the transient respite from the intense heat. Outside is still the same dry, barren wasteland with the mob of swarming traffic, but inside is calm, whitewashed buildings are adorned with colourful floral and ivy, and the contours of the grounds are choking with vibrant green shrubs. I'm surprised to cycle straight into the path of a group of American tourists and their impressive collection of North Face attire, they genuinely looked prepared for a full-scale desert expedition. They asked me where I was going and where I'd come from. They're on a tour through central Rajathan, their guide pamphlets in one hand, cameras in the other. One guy tells me, 'man I wish I was in shape to do something like this', rubbing and patting his robust, paunchy stomach under his 'Expedition Desert' shirt, 'good on you kid!'.

I'm offered a room for the night by the ashram. There's no electricity, I write notes in my journal by headtorch, the stucco walls are mint green and crumbling like old fresco, I hear music coming from downstairs. I head down and taking off my shoes, step into the pale marble floored prayer hall. I gain attention when I walk inside as the only white westerner there. I follow a young boy, he can't be older than twelve years old, he bends and touches the floor as he walks in, touching his chest and then the back of his large, floppy ears, I kneel down behind him, his eyes are shut tight, as if concentrated to grip hold of his faith. The music that fills the room is transcending, elating and the sound reverberates around the walls adorned with detailed illustrations of ancient Hindu stories and teachings. I feel incredibly at peace and happy, confidant in such an alien place, deserving almost, isolated in this strange location which is just another temple off the side of the highway, the main archery from Rajasthan to the west coast and Mumbai. I stay there for some time and then sit and listen to some incoherent mantras in that magical Hindi tongue. When I leave, the sun has almost set. A pink and purple glaze bleeds across scattered clouds. The scene is set, in the foreground is an abandoned concrete shack covered in an armour of ivory and soft moss in the middle of some overgrown garden, a flock of white Cormorants sweep over top. It's my scene, all my own, my own little perfect sunset somewhere amongst the endless dry fields of corn and mustard seeds. There is constant hum and clattering of metal from the highway and the whining sound of bulging tires still hangs in the background. I gave thanks at this moment for the endless treats that travel brings and for the rewards that comes from persistently hacking away at a monotonous daily routine.

*

It's sometimes easy to allow physical surroundings dictate your mood and feelings. Who wouldn't feel less optimistic when looking at a swamp filled with faeces, plastic and animal hind. But this must not affect how I feel in my heart towards this country. Maybe this is India. Maybe this is one of the huge cultural differences. Their attention and love and devotion to spirit, gods, gurus, heads so up in the air that they forget the mound building up around their ankles. It's one of India's many beautiful paradox's.

Mumbai

Life is full of random, bizarre experiences, especially when out on the road, which winds spontaneously day to day. This feels like absolute joy when travelling, and part of the ever-flowing river of experience which takes on so many routes and detours if you go openly, willingly, freely, but you must go this way. If existence allows it to happen, let it happen, flow with it, before the mind interrupts, rationalises, becomes an obstacle. Sometimes you just got to 'go with the flow'.

*

I was invited to a club in Mumbai's financial district. The tall, glossy black buildings dominated the skies, the entrance to the club was guarded and security in neat black suits sat slumped at their posts, one was watching a street vendor push his squeaking popcorn and tobacco cart down the dark street, how paradoxically out of place he looked. The club was a riot of what looked like India's elite, dressed up in the finest suits and dresses and drinking martini cocktails at the bar, I sat in the corner, with my spare, sandy shorts and a cheap shirt I brought from the market earlier that morning, sandals were the only footwear alternatives I had to my cycle shoes, I felt instantly out of place, but couldn't care less. My friends arrived, and we had one beer before leaving, I was very grateful seeing as one was

75

the price of a large meal of cheap guesthouse. We were joined by a pilot, who invited us to his hotel room near the top floor of the building for more drinks, we relaxed on huge comfy sofas and looked out over the city from the comfort of a luxury air-conditioned suit with room service, marble sinks and automatic espresso machines.

One of them was a young graphics designer who boasted of designing some of the best luxury apartments in Mumbai. The pilot was short, stocky man and spoke rapidly about his difficult training program as a pilot, he paced the room continuously sipping on a glass of whisky, he said he was flying tomorrow morning so he couldn't drink past eleven o'clock otherwise he'll fail the breathalyzer test. He said this with some well versed conviction. They asked me about all the places I had been to get here, some of which they'd never heard of and most of which they had never been, all they knew was the city they grew up in.

I looked over a city still breathing hard, still trying, my senses were alive for the world behind that glass, I could still smell that land, and I could still hear sounds of a hot Indian night flowing up through the air in layers, the sounds of a city that never sleeps, car horns and steam, drums and crickets, the sound of people getting up, weak and holding on, working day and night, but never giving up.

I took a Taxi ride back. I'm in an alternative world here, a world so far from the one I born into, I love this feeling of surrendering to the swing of a wild, alien world. This is

Bombay, a place set back in time, yet conditioned and worn by the rapid pace of things. To be in Mumbai is to witness the ultimate dichotomy of life in a major city of a developing country. It's India's financial capital, a place of skyscrapers, air-conditioned shopping centre's and coffee chains, and it's a place where palm trees still slouch in dark corners across the city. It's a place where wet and dry garbage, rotten vegetables and mobile phone cases are moulded onto the baking street surfaces. It's a place you can drink a cold beer and chat with entrepreneurs at a luxury rooftop restaurant smoking shisha, whilst looking down onto a slum below.

My young taxi driver with his spindly neck and handlebar moustache tells me 'no speak English, only Hindi', he mumbles it as an end to any further discussion it's a phrase he rarely uses, and starts his aggressive driving, into the humid, heady night air wrestling with the steering wheel like some captain of a ship in heavy seas. His driving style is terrible, rapid and careless, using no particular lane and only pushing through whatever spaces are available as fast as his little squeaky cab will take him. This is more like a real life Mario cart game.

I indicated to the driver to stop, paid him and walked straight into a local bar next to my guesthouse. The many bars in Mumbai are scenes straight from a H.S.Thomson or Kerouac novel, smoky low lit rooms glazed with smoke and empty rum bottles, it's evening now and the city turns into the bars for slurry conversations over the day's gossip. Shopkeepers and students relax, folding their arms over their girlfriends as bar staff light their cigarettes as they watch the latest sports update and cricket highlights on the TV's surrounding the bar.

*

Down the dark swell of a backstreet, a toxic, infectious smell lingers in the air. I walk past and glance down the sinister looking street, the air was so murky it looked like metallic haze was hovering over the ground, the tower blocks glisten in the background. The floor is strewn with garbage, pools of infected, stagnant water and trampled mounds of weed. A tall silhouetted body limps across the unlit street. I can just about make out a few features, he's definitely shoeless, his shorts and vest are black, his right foot is horribly disfigured, twisted and folded in on itself so that he walks on the side of it, continuously crushing the worn tissue with every step, it looks like an excruciating act. He is homeless, most probably intoxicated with cheap narcotics, and he suddenly passes out of view into the mouth of a concealed building, swallowed by the night. I pause to think about this man in this derelict alleyway, in this random, wasteful spit of city evolution. I can't help but be stymied by a moral and judgmental wall. I can't help but think that this alleyway with its drunk limping silhouette and intoxicating smells of cattle hind, waste, corrosive metal, and kerosene fumes, this back-washed experiment at the mercy of a rapidly developing city that moves inexorably forward without the slightest consideration for those left behind, the unsuccessful trials of life caught in the uprising of an abundantly affluent city, the dichotomy of wealth and poverty. I'm trying my hardest not to devalue his life in comparison to mine, and have to remind myself that we were both born into the same world but are subjects of different environments; me from a contrastingly wealthy middle class family in England, and him from the clotted backstreets somewhere on the outskirts of a thriving city that moves forward irrespective of his poverty stricken life. These unfiltered, unmediated encounters expose me to the real world, and I am incredibly grateful for that. No longer carried along blindly to the ignorant and idealized, singular view of the world outside my country. Not constantly distracted by all the TV quiz shows and eclectic mix of celebrity panelists discussing the latest gossip, that the world is just fine as long as you're hooked on the latest soaps and dramas. Not to be pessimistic, but to be aware, appreciative of my condition and geography as a human being, to know what's real, what's fake and what's just colourfully distracting you from the truth of our wonderful planet and the conditions of its people.

Hardship

'And I also know how important it is in life not necessarily to be strong but to feel strong, to measure yourself at least once, to find yourself at least once in the most ancient of human conditions, facing blind, deaf stone alone, with nothing to help you but your own hands and your own head'
- *Primo Levi*

I set up the tent in the cold by headtorch. My arms, back and legs ache and all I want to do is fall to the ground and sleep. The routine becomes very laborious as the months roll by. I wake at dawn as the sun starts to pierce the canvas and start changing layers of clothing inside the cramped tent. Small daily tasks became separate challenges themselves. I start rolling up my sleeping bag into its super compact shell with my thinning arms, roll up my sleeping matt, brush my teeth with a toothbrush snapped in half, pack my toiletries away, clean the stove, haul the panniers onto the bike, stretch the cable wires around the frame, continuously catching them on my fingers or thwacking me in the legs or face, refill my water, a quick change of socks (if I'm lucky I'll not be wearing the same pair for three weeks), shoes on, quick stretch, time to go. I'm exhausted before I've even started!

Despite my tiredness I wake up every day with a bubbling excitement for the new day ahead. As I step out of the tent, the noises and the heat and the fusion of smells hits my senses and I feel utterly charmed by this rare place that I chose to be.

My physical and psychological limits were of course thoroughly tested at times. During a scorching week on one of Rajasthan's endless highways, food poisoning proved riding incredibly difficult and I struggled to get up and on the bike. After spending twenty-four hours bedridden and folded in pain over a toilet in a mouldy hotel, without any assistance from painkillers or antibiotics, I still felt seriously ill. My stomach knotted and groaned, I winced in crippling agony, the last thing I wanted to do was to ride a bike. I pushed on regardless, determined not to let one hundred kilometres slip by and waste a whole day. My belly squelched and throbbed, my head pounded and my temperature swung between hot and cold progressively. After forcing myself to eat what I could, which was hardly a few spoonfuls of rice and some water, i'd make it a few kilometers and then throw up on the side of the road or drop my shorts and squat and wait for the acidic burn of waste to spill out of me. Wincing in pain and dripping with sweat, I jumped back on the seat, gritting my teeth, 'Don't you fu**ing stop, Jack, don't you dare!' I would repeat to myself over and over in my mind as the heat continued to sap all my strength. I told myself that I'd encounter moments like this and that it's a vitally important step in my ride. Ultimately, I wouldn't be doing this if it didn't include difficulty, or some level of challenge that would put me in my place, weak and hurting in some wild place with no option but to get my head down keep going, testing the furthest parts of my resolve and mental stamina. I derive a sort of masochistic pleasure from telling my body not to stop, and testing this ongoing battle with the brain. When I'm in that moment of struggle all I want to do is stop, but when I look back, it's where I dig out my increasing strength of character and my ability to push through the boundaries I never thought I could.

*

Countless towns strewed across this hot gulf of dry land have a dystopian, almost apocalyptic quality. It seems as though a sudden and short-lived surge in industry has injected life into the streets. Maybe some people got rich and the community started to prosper but over time the decaying architectural bones of a once thriving town is disappearing, being swallowed once again by the desert. A once whitewashed block of buildings dotted throughout a clustered town is now permeated with mould and peeling paint, faded political slogans, and posters, ultimately forgotten in the backdrop of a colorful fruit market. A cacophony of hectic dialogue and squabble merges in a static wave of ancient and unfamiliar tongue as locals mingle and ply over eminent stacks lucid coloured fruit and veg like guava, oranges, grapes, mangoes and bananas. Some traders are toting coal fires lined with sweet-corn, wafting them with newspaper. I see one woman give one slightly burnt corn to a small begging child with matted hair and snot covering his upper lips, the gold corn turned dark like teeth of the poor burning black.

Behind the confines of these small villages, an endless stretch of land, burnt out by the relentless sun is waiting for me. Out there is my destination, out there is where I must go, this is my route. I become indifferent to the fear of future challenges, events which I have no current control over, I tell myself to relax and enjoy the moment knowing that I'll deal with it when the time comes. And It's at these times where my courage and strength is tested, here lies the real challenge. No alternative way, no easy way, no half measures and I tell myself what an incredibly exciting challenge I'm enduring, tinged with nervousness and a willing ambition to dive unprepared into the unknown. What's also reassuring and thrilling, is to think, how many more days have I got ahead of me like this one, there are still hundreds of days left on this journey, countless more fresh days of wonder and discovery, and beyond this trip? Surely much more, a door has opened and I've started to savour the world on the other side. I push on with my legs burning in pain, tight in the hips and knees, yet strong and extending my pace as I breathe in the fresh air of every new mile.

Purpose

'Do not grow old, no matter how long you live. Never cease to stand like curious children before the great mystery in which we were born' - *Albert Einstein*

It's not about where to travel, it's about how and why. The purpose of this adventure is not strictly about milage or destination, it's more the essence that binds them together. I started out on this journey as an invitation to myself, to enrol in an unprecedented life of exotic adventure, out of my comfort zone and into an ocean of unknown challenges. It was the purpose to find myself in strange, unthinkable places, treading alien territory and embracing an openness to a world so vastly different from the one I knew.

*

I've been off the bike now for nearly two weeks and I'm struggling to remain happy and retain the same energy that was so apparent and surging insatiably through me when I was on the bike. After around two thousand miles I decided to take a small break from the ride in Goa and enjoy life at a slower pace. It's reminding me how easy and relaxing it is to travel backpacking style, just like everyone else. Having the opportunity to lay around in the same spot all day, drink beer, play cards, be sucked into wi-fi spots and be enrolled into a digital duel off with phones and laptops. I'd become lazy, slouchy, flabby, and beyond the lack of physical challenge, a waning lack of purpose startled to settle in.

I had become another roaming backpacker, clean clothed and fresh faced, well rested and comfortable, travelling by air-conditioned bus, utterly unaware of the hellish road conditions, the intense heat, the aggressive accents and stretching kilometres and their effects on the body and mind. I missed that. I missed the sense of challenge. My purpose, the odd joy of hardship and the daring attitude that is fresh and energised in the mind with cycling across an alien country not knowing where the day will take you or where you'll sleep.

I even miss my appearance; dusty, scraggly hair, dry and splayed across my hot temple in the sun, the sunken, lagging skin under my eyes from rough nights sleeping in a tent, the dirt and sweat encrusted tops that rub and stick to my chest and that beaming light of childlike enthusiasm stretched across my face, that rapt expression and glint in my eyes.

I'd much prefer to attempt something incredibly tough and glorious rather than tread the comfortable path of normality. I'd rather try it and then fail, at least I know I gave it my all and that I've only myself to blame. Mastering the control of my life and its accomplishments, knowing that I only failed because of my lack of dedication and weakness and succeeded due to my determination and effort. I want to take full control of my life. I want to take it back!

Perception

'The most dangerous risk of all is spending your life not doing what you want on the bet that you can buy yourself the freedom to do it later' - *Randy Komisar*

We are always looking forward. Planning for the future, often contributing so much of our precious time and energy in constructing the blueprint of a secure and financially stable future. The price of anything is how much time we exchange for the action, time we cannot get back. We have become so focused on getting up the shore that we can become oblivious to the whole ocean behind us, heads down so much they miss the sun rising over the peaks.

When you're constantly focused on the future, living in the future, you're consciously repressing and forgetting this moment right now, this glorious present moment. The sounds of crickets in my ears, the smell of warm sand and petrol. You miss the beauty and grace of what's right in front of you. With small steps not only will you come to relish and thrive in your current moment, but all your thoughts and feelings for the future will change, you'll be connected to something greater within you which recognizes and listens to your true identity, passions and ambitions. We're always being told to work hard, to stop dreaming all the time, but we keep proving them wrong by choosing this open path, this unique, individual, self-directed path which floods the body with an surge to live as richly as possible and finally accept the life you want to live.

We need to learn to pull away the rocks held in place by society that are preventing our rivers from flowing. I urge you to smash away at the surface of your damn that preventing all that water from flooding the dry, starving planes that lie before you waiting for the water, waiting for spring, the nourishment it needs to flourish into a beautiful oasis, ripe in colour, sound and so much life. The man-made space between your dreams and your reality must be challenged! Your gut feeling should take priority over your life, and overcome the more conditioned actions (or actions not taken) by your head, your logic, your reasoning and your inhibitions.

Palm Wine and Night Riding

'If you have built castles in the sky, your work not need be lost; that is where they should be. Now put foundations under them' - *H. Thoreau*

In the state of Gujarat, situated the north-west corner of the country, the government enforced strict prohibition on all alcohol trade across the county in an attempt to improve the health and productivity of its people. Yet, the Gujaratis, find a way around it, naturally. Sporadically spaced out across the dry plains and often just on the shoulder of the main highway are local tribeswomen with nothing but a few plastic chairs, a 50 litre plastic bucket and a tray of glasses. These are pit stops for drivers wishing to have an afternoon tipple of Palm wine or, 'Kallu', a cheap and easy to produce alcoholic drink often made in people's farms and backyards. The trees bark is slashed and the sap from the bark is collected and then fermented producing a foul, sour taste with hints of acidic white wine. I stopped to observe one of these small stalls in action when a few truck drivers approached me and invited me for a taste. Being a dry state, I hadn't had drink in a few weeks, so the sickly, white liquid worked its magic in just a few minutes. More drivers turned up and I felt obliged to join them as they offered me more wine. After an hour of storytelling, mostly aided with sign action and photos from my mobile, I felt too tired and drowsy to cycle on. I had been determined throughout this trip not to have any help from any other vehicles or lifts along the way, wanting to cycle every inch of the way, so when they offered me a lift all the way to Mumbai, a distance of about 90 kilometres I was staggered, facing a moral dilemma that I thought might pollute the essence of my journey. Then I reminded myself that this trip was about experiencing as much as I could, saying yes to all the unique opportunities that come my way, and so I convinced myself that it would only add to my list of amusing discoveries that had already become an abundant list.

We attached a rope to the bike and hauled it up in the back of a large TaTa lorry. These lorries are in abundance across the entire country and are used for transporting all manner of goods. The inside of the cabin was decked out in an impressive array of tacky decoration, flags, pictures and posters of Hindu gods and sari gladded women bleached colourless from hours of intense sun burning through the cabin on its many long hauls. The horn was hilarious with its variation of loud jingles, as was the stereo and it's one loud setting. The two drivers sang along constantly the crackling, distorted songs in their Gujurati language. They would keep checking with me to see if I knew every new song that came on, which of course I didn't. The cabin was spacious enough to lie down in and I slouched back, exhausted, rested my feet on the window ledge, letting the cool breeze air my stinking feet. The big, hard sun burnt down on the dry plains, over wide, flat land, barren and beaten by the intense sun. I saw the occasional dwelling amongst the fields where skinny farmers, heads wrapped in cloth protecting them from the sun pulled camels with rope across the land, haltered to their necks and from their ring pierced noses. The smell of animal hind was almost tangible.

After a few hours of driving and a handful of fascinated glares from passing drivers who saw me in the cab of a local lorry with two Indians dancing to and singing with our arms in the air, we finally came to a stop in the middle of the highway, a quick chai stop I thought maybe. A squeak from the brakes and a hiss from the engine and we pulled over onto the sandy bank off the road. A bloated tire swung from a sad looking tree and an unlit garage was lurking ominously a few meters away from the road. 'You leave now', they said, 'we go, different road, not Mumbai'. My face dropped with shock at this news, but then turned again into a smile, a sort of amusing nod, typical India I told myself, nothing ever goes as planned here. I stood on top of the lorry and attached the rope to the frame of my bike and started to lower it down.

On top of a lorry, on a hot Indian night, to the smell of hot sand and car fumes, trampling boxes of unknown cargo over thick tarpaulin, to the silence of a desert, interrupted by other lorries screaming past at high speed as waves of light hit my face. This really felt like an adventure. I lowered the bike down to the ground, and watched as the lights of the lorry passed beyond sight leaving me in the edge of a lightless highway with no idea where to go or how far it was to the next town.

My stomached squelched with hunger, I was crashing from lack of carbohydrates after the rest of the day's ride. The highway is mobbed by loud cars and lorry's that whizz past as I push on unknowingly down the long, dark highway. After an hour of riding, the only places I found along the way were expensive, air-conditioned hotels that wanted to charge £40 pounds per night, an impossible task given my £5 a day budget. I moved further towards the distant lights of a big city, uprising and sparkling in the hot night of the Indian desert. A man on his motorbike rode alongside me for a few minutes and chatted to me on the move, which at first, I found incredible irritating due to my exhaustion, but was then suddenly enjoying the company when he suggested attaching my bike lock to the back of his bike so that he could pull me along at a safe distance. We coasted for another half an hour before reaching the next town, an expensive suburb of Mumbai. I thanked the man immensely for his help and advice on where to look for cheap accommodation and then went straight away in search of food and a cold beer. It was 11:00pm by this time and I had started the day at 8:00am. I went into a nearby restaurant, flanked by giant, black palms wrapped in flashing neon lights. All the men inside looked different, I was near the city, closer to money and you could tell, they were nearly all fat! They quarrel and laughed for hours, sipping on beers and whisky, smoking cigarettes and watching the cricket highlights on the surrounding TV's. I ordered gooey spring rolls, egg fried rice, chips and a large beer.

The food sent me into a deep slumber. I found myself fixated on the cricket game, with almost no energy to move, slumping further and further into the chair. My eyes started to close, feeling the deep need to rest, and drawing in those deep breathes of air just before sleep, only to be awaken by the sudden bursts of laughter from the groups of drunk men in the corners of the restaurant. By this time it was well past midnight, I know I wouldn't find anywhere cheap to stay in the this seemingly expensive district outside of Mumbai and the thought of searching for somewhere, riding to multiple places, negotiating prices and arguing the occasional cocky receptionist made me even more tired. I accepted my fate of sleeping rough for this night. I hauled my heavy bike from the reception area and started to look for somewhere reasonably quiet and safe where I could sleep. I pondered behind cars deep down dark roads, gaps in the fields on the side of the road, fenced and lightless. I finally stumbled upon a car park around the back of a hotel where a few caretakers were lighting a fire in a dingy garage. They welcomed me in after a few inquisitive questioned and I slept there for the night, on the warm concrete floor next to the fire and the constant, low chattering of the three kind strangers. The sound of a gigantic city hung in the background like a soft, all-encompassing mist.

Heading south

'The notion of travel as a continuous vision, a grand tour's succession of memorable images across a curved earth - with none of the distorting emptiness of air or sea'
- *P. Theroux*

South India is now fully apparent and showing off its colours. A new cacophony of sights, smells and sounds flood my periphery, such is my reward for sticking to a monotonous routine.

The narrow roads wind through wild and uncultivated palm groves where giant plants and vines straight from a scene of Jurassic park entwine with electric cables. The people are dark and muscular with white teeth and warm coloured saris. Flower petals and coconut husks appear on the russet coloured earth next to the road.

People walk barefoot on cracked soles, the women are incredibly pretty and impeccably dressed schoolgirls decorate their platted hair with festoons of yellow jasmine. The sun is fierce and the air is perfumed with the smell of fish, coconut oil, flowers from the temples, cinnamon and sea salt. The thousand mile stretch of coastline running vertically south along the western coast means you are hardly ever out of sight of the Arabian sea. I catch glimpses of a burnished ocean through the palm trees, and often end my day turning off the main highway and down a side street, which often, after just a few kilometers, takes me straight to the beach. I follow the smell of sea salt and fish, and little fish stalls and rickshaws with carts of polystyrene boxes filled with ice and lucid coloured fish pop up just a few hundred meters from the sea. They waft the flies away with newspaper. The humidity is unbearable and sweat beads drop one by one from my nose, sometimes in silent couplets like suicide pact tears jumping together. Salt sweat gets in my eyes and I try to remove it with my knuckles whilst avoiding the incessant onslaught of traffic, my gloves are encrusted with snot and sweat. It's just one of the many daily challenges I have to endure on this blistering journey.

If there's ever an opportunity to swim or wash in fresh water, I quite literally *jump* at the chance. One afternoon, I pass a bridge over a wide, muddy river park my bike underneath in the shade and head down the bank hastily stripping off my clothes, dumping them on a rock and then diving straight into the cool, murky water in my underpants There are some repairs being made to the bridge and a small group of men throwing bowls of sand from above their heads and into cement mixers stop to point and wave. The slow current drifts me along and under the bridge like a log where I pass into the shade and cling onto one of the bridges foundations covered in slimy algae. I lie in the shade and let the water wash over me in the immense heat. My attitude has changed along this trip. My natural, excited inclination tells me to keep pushing out the miles and cover as much distance as possible, but I remind myself of the importance of slowing down and savoring this special journey that I am enduring.

As I get out and wade my way through the deep muddy banks that forever swallow my feet, I see three young boys on bikes waiting for me. They are giddily excited to see me in their small town and I let each one have a go on my bike. They carry slabs of ice on the back of their bikes, which is quickly melting in the sun. They break some up with a rock and give me a slab of ice, it was such a simple gesture of generosity. Very grateful for this little offering of cold ice, I dropped it into my hat and crushed it with the base of my foot. I wave them goodbye as I take off, *'chello, chello',* melting ice trickling down my face and cooling my neck in a river of ice-cold water. I continue to pound the pedals and the heavy load of the bike into the heat.

*

I pull up at a tea shack next to a slum, desperate to get out of the scorching sun. I don't see anybody and I shout, 'chai, chai'. A woman pops up from behind some terracotta cooking pots, hiding her face shyly behind her maroon sari. She turns on the kerosene cooker, crushes some ginger and carda
mon and spoons in some sugar. She passes me a plastic chair and hands me the chai lifting her sari back over her shoulder, she's shoeless and cautious as she walks, her fingers are covered in red, spiraling henna. I admire the incredible detail, her fingernails that are painted dark red. She doesn't say a word

*

I set my tent up in the back gardens of a restaurant and then sit and read my book on a squeaky swing, cobwebs hanging from the rusting brackets above from years of unuse. As I sit there swinging an unseen train suddenly turns the silent hills into a rhythmic clattering of metallic voices. I think I catch glimpses of it through the bushy foliage in the distance.

This is the main train route between Mumbai and Goa and is therefore most likely carrying tired, sluggish tourists, utterly unaware that I am here, in my own garden flanked with palm trees and choked by blushing red Rhododendrons, my little battered tent tied down to the packed, russet earth.

I'd love to see it from the train myself. Catching split second glimpses, through the trees of a western looking male, standing amongst the mass density of a forest. My features would certainly be unclear they would definitely make out a smile radiating from that scene. They might lose me between the trees for a moment and then catch another glimpse through the foliage. In that moment I play imaginative games as to what they would be thinking overlooking that scene and am reminded again of where I am on this adventure and why I'm here. A wanderer, a thrill seeker, tracing through new territory, cast out from a voice long ago that spoke bravely about undergoing some long adventure all by himself, words which were no more than brave idle words caught up in the head of someone who just wanted to go!

The people in the train continue to eat peanuts and slouch into a sweaty slumber, thundering towards the beach party awaiting them in Goa.

I continue swinging happily, catching my heals in the sand and enjoying the sound of pistachio coloured parrots squawking in the trees over my head.

Chair with a Crown. A Rich Man

'Loving life is easy when you're abroad. Where no one knows you and you hold your life in your hands all alone, you are more master of yourself than ever before'
- Hannah Arendt

I love the feeling of freedom that comes with simply being in momentum, flowing through life, flowing with an energy unconditioned, undirected and unrestricted. I'm on the move again, somewhere new, thousands of miles have already been covered, with yet more to go. The day is blisteringly hot and the tarmac sweats. I smile over the passing road as it's mottled surface is chewed up by the bike mile after mile and I relish the day, a fresh day, the only day to truly enjoy and embrace, looking out with childlike enthusiasm and piecing together fragments of forever changing India. Palm trees start to perch out from the roadside; the world's oldest travellers.

*

My world before in England was very different. I was caught up in my environment, and the norms of how people around me were acting. I would enroll in the consumer paradise, working in sober reliance to my job commitments only to dive into a splurge of wasteful short lived self-indulgence, fettering myself further to more material things. All these external qualities were the plastic fruits of my toiled labour; new clothes, a new watch, a new magazine subscription I never read and lunches at

Starbucks. I would feel the temporary sense of fulfillment whenever I purchased something that I wanted, or was persuaded to buy by clever marketing that makes you feel incomplete or left out if you don't have it.

The fruits of my labour are different on the road, what I gain in return for my efforts is different, more real, more substantial, more memorable and richer than any *thing* that I could buy with money. Nothing that you ever buy will make you whole. True fulfillment comes at the end of the day, when you sit in silence, totally exhausted, with a plate full of food you sweated over all day and a soul bubbling with what it has seen and felt. It's when you revel in the accomplishments of a challenging day, the new experiences and the simple joys of a day so vastly different from the last, knowing full well that tomorrow will be different.

*

I set my tent up in the garden of an expensive highway hotel, the grass is the greenest I've seen for some time. Exhausted, I slump against one of the many palm trees that line the garden, the trunk is a spiral flare of spiky callous arms but a patch just big enough for my sweaty back is smoothed out at its base. It's my own perfect chair, complete with a wide tropical crown. I watch the last few slides of sun dip beneath the surrounding field of palms with a cold beer and a bag of fresh oranges by my side.

The whole scene is mine, it's perfect and I've earned it. What a perfect end to another perfect day I tell myself. I gulp down a giant piece of orange and listen to the birds nestling in the low tree canopies along with the constant hum of traffic from the highway behind me. The warmth of the sun coats my dry, dirty face.

My day has been so simplistic and yet so fulfilling. I feel like the richest man in the world, having spent my day working hard and with a purpose, watching this glorious sunset through tired eyes and smiling, knowing that I have spent my day in the best way possible.

Simplicity

'Simplify, simplify, simplify' - *H. Thoreau*

I enjoy the simplicity and purpose of my days. None of the other typical, daily worries that we might burden ourselves with, getting to work on time, making calls to people you don't like, pushing back the emails, none of these concern me. All I have to do is cycle a certain distance, find food and shelter, that's all. If I do these things, then I have lived my day well. It may not seem like much, but to me accomplishing these things gave me a huge sense of fulfillment, and ultimately they have taken me further towards my goal, to the end of India. It seems that the more we do and the more we think creates a multitude of layers in the mind, these layers may seem useful, practical they may help with our daily lives, with our blossoming careers, but they are still nothing more than added weight to our already heavy, mental load. The simplicity of cycling everyday had an opposite effect, it allowed me to let go. By letting go I opened myself up change, I unburdened myself from the past and from the world I knew, towards the world unknown.

*

My room at home is full of stuff. Stuff I don't need, don't use and don't even remember. Folds of paper here, a plastic case there, a bag of something, a draw of things, a stack of more stuff and behind that more lost limbs of abandoned objects, more things, more stuff collecting dust. And what are possessions but things we hold onto in fear that we will need them tomorrow?

Everything I carry with me on this cycle I need, everything has a purpose and everything has a place. A wise man once said that the things that you own, end up owning you. Out here I had little ownership. I have some warm clothes, a tent, a camera and a notepad. The knowledge of this allowed a lighter mental load too, I wasn't distracted by any other materialistic wants, I simply carried things I needed to survive and stretch forward day by day. A gloriously sweaty and dirty penance to materialism.

Living within these means also gave great importance to seemingly meaningless items; a scrap piece of metal wire that I used to bind my front left pannier to the bike frame, the salvaged tape and the small cube of rubber that stopped the bags rattling on the brackets. All these small things have great significance.

I set up camp one evening looking up the valley into the lofty, snow peaked summits not far away. An empty, raised patch of soil and stone on the side of the winding mountain road is the perfect size for my tent. A local invites me into his house and to escape the bitter cold for an exotic feast of vodka and corn flakes. I sway back a few hours later up the path towards my little green tent perched quietly on the ridge. I have my own little world by camping outside, my own 5 billion star hotel, I say to myself 'my life is fucking fantastic!', so rich, so memorable, so fragrant, so joyous, so alert and alive. These are the memories and experiences in which real life and real meaning is found. The air is silent except for the small sound of a river bellowing far below and I can just make out the jagged mountain peaks in the distance as the moon sheds light over them giving them a posthumous white glow under the stars. My warm breath billowing out warm air in wisps of smoke.

The world became a place to sit and hug tired knees at the end of a long day watching changing light. I sat on the shoulders of the earth as life slowed. I chose simplicity. Accompanied only by nature and my thoughts, or perhaps my lack of them. It's funny how exposing yourself to new and exciting environments and feasting upon the curiously of what's around the next corner is a great way to turn the brain from its addiction to thinking laterally. The world carried on blindly, the cities still roared, their pace quickened, their feet stamped, shaking the ground, marking their place. My grace deepened. A sudden flashback of another tedious office meeting polluted my mind, then I came back to where I was, under some black tarpaulin roof of a small tea bazaar. An elderly man was crushing ginger on a concave slab of wood, the floor covered in nutshells and the shelves filled with mangoes and coconuts, I sipped the edge of a steaming glass of chai, raising it to the fading sun in a 'cheers' action and screamed an incredulous burst of joy inside my heart.

*

Sun through the trees, straw dwellings in open fields sit amongst abstract pools of glistening water where buffaloes chew methodically in the sun. As I'm cycling I start to see real India again, into the lives of thousands of individuals. One man stands and walks across the back of a moving truck, I just catch his face in a brief moment of panning focus, thundering towards me on the other side of the road, two motorcyclists move closer together on the pine carpeted road so that they can laugh at each other's jokes. A small group of people cling onto the flanks of a tractor, their saris buffeting and flapping in the wind in temporary roar and flash of lucid colour.

India

'This Mother earth, India is very pure. The thought, the feeling, the sentiment is grounded. They talk and act from the heart, not from the head, not so physically; such sentient beings'

India has to be embraced fully, swallowed whole. Because the reality is it's a harsh country, where poverty is strife and life is tough. You damn the world for the poor girls sleeping rough on the street, the amputees pulling themselves down the streets in rich cities, the mothers raising their children in a concrete jungle with nothing but a few rugs for warmth and outstretched hands for food. And then you'll feel a heavy knot of guilt that you are just utterly helpless. You must endure the bad and ugly as *it* does, endure the darkness and embrace the pleasures.

It's a place that shocks and enriches perspective. It's a place to reevaluate and reconsider the fortunate qualities we are encompassed by in the west; money, education, privileges, infrastructure, distributed healthcare. For me it also held the ability to jolt my perception on the things that *we* can learn from the eastern world, undamaged beauty, hearts as open as fountains, the celebrations of this mysterious life through the acts of worship and creativity, the wandering mystic minds that push on into the unknown, outside the confines of work, status, wealth and possessions. I have a lot to thank India for.

*

I threaded my bike through the mass crowds of a festival in
Jaipur, Rajasthan.

In the small streets, several local women cladded in brass
coloured saris carry huge, ambiguous lamps above their heads,
as they walk towards the town centre. All the lights are linked
with cables leading to a generator that follows them behind in a
rickshaw. They sway through streets in their portable phantoms
of light kicking through waste and around cows as they head
towards the festival. A surge of light and sound and their gone,
deep into the winding night.

I walked a little further and stopped by a lake, stooped on a
ledge covered in moss and incense ash and looked quietly over
the still water. The sage coloured lake spanned the vast, flat
plains, only stopping at amorphous edges of distant hills, above
which a mauve sky hung, so lovely it looked scented. I saw this
beautiful accumulation of waste form in some rut on the lower
steps leading to the water's edge, next to soft, cream coloured
Egrets, black-throated Kingfishers and Swallows. The washed
up detritus came from a combination of Puja's (acts of worship
including flowers and candles), and general waste that breeds
on the water surface: broken clay pots, flower heads, glass,
shards of plastic and forgotten jewellery, all shattered and
scattered upon the wet rocks, used and then forgotten, thrown
back into the chaotic, endless pattern of life. There is beauty in
this chaos I'm looking at, in the material melee, amongst the

overtaking tide of nature; I thought how India is such a place. This huge variety of strange and colourful materials coming together and forming a unity, whose meaning and history is far behind my understanding, but whose beauty is undisputable and surrealy poetic. Again, I thought about India, her colour and intensity, her fragrance and harshness, her chaos and her charm, India is such a place.

Ending at The Ocean

'The sea's only gifts are harsh blows, and occasionally, the chance to feel strong' - *Primo Levi*

Finishing at the sea feels very concluding, sealed to approval by the sea of infinity. It seems like the right way to finish an adventure. You've reached the end of a long hard road, and know you can go no further; only sea. It is the end, yet the start of something else.

The last day brought with it yet more challenges. My cable gear snapped 200km from the finish, six months on the road and it happens now, yet more resistance from the spirit of adventure and her relentless obstacles. I use all the strength I have left to keep the wheels turning – my knees and thighs throbbing with pain.

The day is hot under the cruel April sun. I pick up the pace, counting down the kilometers to 'Kanyakumari' the most southerly town in India, 298, 135, 111, 93km.
I am hidden from the sea or any sight of the end. It's just another busy day on the bike, down roads choked with traffic and dry shrub punctuated with palm groves, and the frequent 'BEEEEEEEEPEPEEEEPEPEEEP'. I had spent six months making this my daily routine, my new home to explore, it had become my life, and now mile by mile I was bringing it to a close.

I take a final chai stop before the last stretch and talk a little longer to the lady who works there. I know I won't have these lucky little interactions for much longer. I tip her and thank her greatly for her delicious tea and wave as I ride off.

I'm exhausted and my skin burns from the incredible heat. I tell myself to take my time and enjoy this final leg but I'm excited and determined to finish this journey. I stretch out the miles and the last few hours seem never ending.

I enter into the coastal town that hosts my finish. No one is waiting for me, no friends, family or press are going to be there. I am alone, just the way I want it to be. I push through another busy street market and work my way through a swarm of dark skinned people shopping and sipping tea in the shade of canvas chai stalls. A few miles back I brought a large Indian flag from a souvenir shop and draped it across the rear of my panniers. I had been cycling through the town for a few miles mile now and there was still no sign of the end.

And then, just moments later, I saw it. The flat horizon was suddenly broken by a open line of blue sea. The finish line was in sight. I passed through a police check and down a narrow-cobbled path towards the sea.

I took the flag off the bike and punched it in the air, raising it high above my head as it flapped wildly in the sea breeze for all to see.

The sense of pride and unbridged affection for this special place in the world ran through all my veins and into some untouched part of my being, rooting way down into my guts, three thousand miles flashed before my eyes, the places, the challenges, the people, the intense and euphoric feeling burning through every animated cell in my body.

I rode until I could ride no more. The road had finally ended. I was absolutely exhausted. An amphitheatre of steps led down onto the beach in front of huge, crashing waves and an ocean with nothing in front of it but bright blue sky. I walked down onto the beach and buried my feet in the cold water. I wrapped the flag around my shoulders and looked out into the deep blue ocean as tears started to roll down my cheek. I cried and cried. I cried over India, over my accomplishment, over the end of this life changing chapter.

Like any adventure the value is in the process, not the finish. But all my efforts had led me to this moment. All the effort, pain, high times, low times the straining and monotonous routine had led me here.

These moments are very special. They remind me why I'm here and the meaning behind a purposeful quest. I have to go back home now. I can't just keep going. Something else waits for me across the water. The importance of this journey is not yet apparent, it's efforts will be realized soon, when I'm home in England – back into the world that I came from, where the tones of adventure will sink deep into my skin and glaze everything in a layer of vibrant curiosity and a newfound admiration for what lies ahead.

All I know is that I want to feed and nurture this new life, to dive into something unprepared and inexperienced and emerge forged, like iron hardened from a furnace of challenging experiences.

It's time to go home and start a new chapter.

~ The End ~

About the Author

Jack Few is an aspiring adventurer, travel writer, photographer and filmmaker. This is his first major expedition and debut novel.

He is currently training for an expedition to cycle The Silk Road; from Europe to Asia.

www.jackfew.com

Your feedback on *An Eastern Tailwind* would really be appreciated:
jackfewtravel2014@gmail.com

Writing, proofreading, editing, marketing (or lack of), design and publishing, by Jack Few. If this book is awful, there's only one person to blame.

Cover design: Jack Few and Alx Green, Matt Sparks. Thanks for your help and sorry for being a pain!

With thanks to Polly Bell for inspiring the publishing name.

Please consider donating this book to a fellow traveler or charity shop when you have finished it.